GarageSale:
The Manual

GarageSale: The Manual

IWASCODING.COM

Cortero Publishing
www.CorteroPublishing.com
An Imprint of Fireship Press

GarageSale: The Manual—Copyright © 2009 by iwascoding GmbH

ISBN-13: 978-1-934757-91-8
ISBN-10: 1-934757-91-8

BISAC Subject Headings:

COM064000 COMPUTERS / Electronic Commerce
BUS090000 BUSINESS & ECONOMICS / E-Commerce
BUS090010 BUSINESS & ECONOMICS / E-Commerce / Internet Marketing

Address all correspondence to:

Fireship Press, LLC
P.O. Box 68412
Tucson, AZ 85737

Or visit our website at:
www.FireshipPress.com

1.0

Contents

INTRODUCTION

About iwascoding

iwascoding is a German company that was founded in 2005. Frustrated by the absence of eBay listing utilities for the Mac OS X the company's founders Ilja Iwas and Paul Hecker created a client application for the eBay online auction system. Today iwascoding is at the forefront in developing outstanding tools to make eBay selling easier for OS X users. The company accounts for approximately 300,000 auctions per month and numbers are increasing. About fifty percent of the company's customers are in the U.S. and forty percent in Germany.

iwascoding received the award for *Best Newcomer Q1/Q2 2005* at eBay's Germany developer day in 2005. Its innovative application, GarageSale, consistently outclasses competitors in magazine tests. *MacWelt Germany* compared eBay listing applications in issue 08/2006 and GarageSale won with the rating "very good." The German Magazine *MacLife* rated GarageSale as the best eBay application twice in issues 06/2005 and 04/2006.

The iwascoding product line consists of four interrelated products:

GarageSale—a slick, full-featured client application for the eBay online auction system—is now one of the leading eBay listing tools for the Mac platform. iwascoding just released *GarageSale 5*, an extensive update to its forerunners.

GarageSale Basic—the smaller brother to its award-winning eBay client. It was developed for customers who don't need all the advanced eBay features its bigger brother provides. GarageSale Basic includes all the essential features for listing on eBay a casual seller dreams about.

GaragePay—a new management tool for PayPal transactions. GaragePay lets you download, view, search, and archive all your PayPal transactions without having to log into the PayPal website. It handles incoming as well as outgoing money transfers.

GarageBuy is the first Mac application featuring eBay-certified bidding functionality. Bids can be placed instantly without having to wait for all those web pages to load. It also features an intuitive Gallery view, which loads as many images from your found items as fit on your screen. You don't have to open each single listing just to see how the item looks anymore. **GarageBuy-Touch,** is the iPhone version of GarageBuy, which allows you to bid at any time, from virtually anywhere.

About Garage Sale

GarageSale is the leading client applications for the eBay online auction system for Mac users. New features such as network sharing, the easy access to YouTube videos and a report generator amend the latest version.

GarageSale is a sophisticated, full-featured client application for the eBay online auction system. It offers advanced features while remaining user friendly. With GarageSale Mac OS X users can compose eye-catching auctions quickly using an intuitive Mac-like interface. GarageSale also integrates perfectly with iPhoto, offers WYSIWYG text editing and comes with over 140 free design templates. All that's required is a Mac OS X 10.4.0 or higher. It is an excellent solution for small to medium-scale eBay sellers.

About this Book

Despite the success of GarageSale, something was missing—a printed manual to tie it all together. From the beginning, iwascoding had an online user manual; but, as the popularity of the product grew, it became clear that that was not enough. People wanted a book. They wanted something that was more portable, that they could read when not at their computers, and place next to them when they were.

This manual is the answer to that need.

We hope that this book will contain all the information you will ever need to operate every aspect of GarageSale. But we also know that no manual has ever accomplished that goal. As a result, iwascoding also maintains a very active *GarageSale User Group* at:

Tech.groups.yahoo.com/Group/GarageSale_Users

There you will find thousands of fellow users, and an enormous pool of practical experience. The message board alone is a veritable encyclopedia of tips, tricks, and problems solved.

Thus, if you have a problem with GarageSale, and the answer can not be found in this manual, and the answer can not be found in the User Group, and the answer can not be found via GarageSale Technical Support—then the answer doesn't exist.

You have bought the finest eBay sales management software in the world.

Use it. Enjoy it. Profit from it!

Getting Started

CHAPTER I
GarageSale Installation and Set-up

Introduction

GarageSale makes it easy for you to sell and manage items on eBay. It simplifies the process of offering items and allows you to quickly create templates speeding up the process of offering similar items in the future. GarageSale offers you more than 1000 layout options. You can also minimize charges by, for example, using GarageSale's Free Picture Service or GarageSale's built-in auction scheduler

Download and Install GarageSale

- Download the GarageSale disk image file (.dmg) from the GarageSale website: www.iwascoding.com /GarageSale.
- Double-click on this .dmg file to view its contents (see next page).
- Drag and drop the GarageSale icon to your *applications folder* to install the application on your hard drive.
- Eject the disk image volume by dragging the volume icon to the trash.
- Open the *applications folder*. Start GarageSale by double- clicking on the icon.

That's all there is to it!

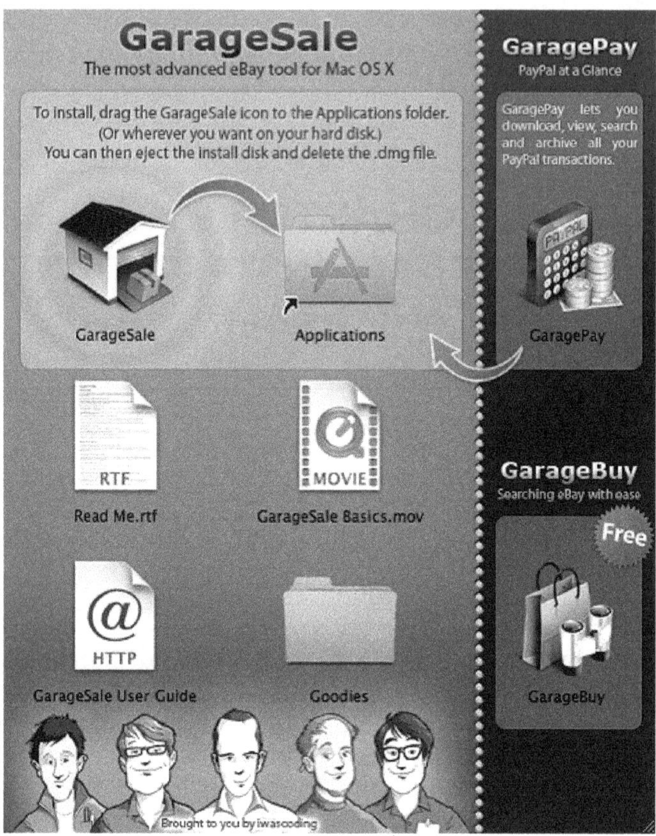

Initial Setup

The welcome window gives you the possibility of trying GarageSale for free (demo) or to purchase it directly. A demo installation allows you to test GarageSale for three auctions. If you need to be convinced, that'll do it! Click Purchase to obtain a license right away.

> **Onward and Upward**
>
> In a single month, March 2009, GarageSale users posted over 400,000 items on eBay.

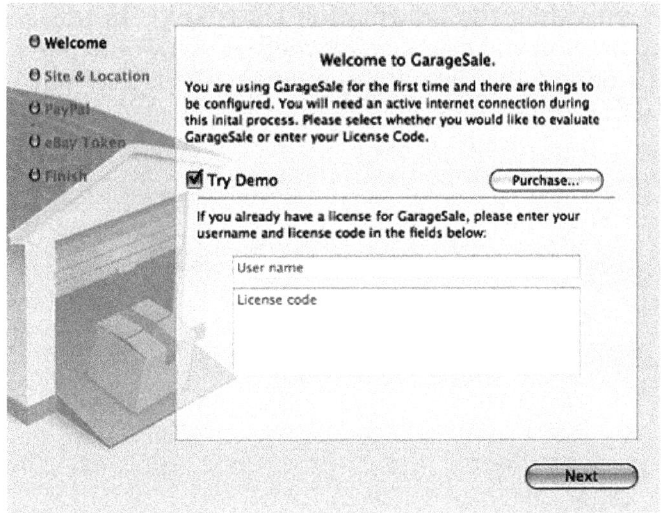

There are several ways to receive your license for GarageSale. Click on any of the buttons among the purchase options to start a dialog that allows you to buy the software.

Press *Next* to choose the eBay site you would like to sell from, and where you are located. You may change the entries for *eBay site*, *country*, *region* and *location* in the *Preferences* window at any time.

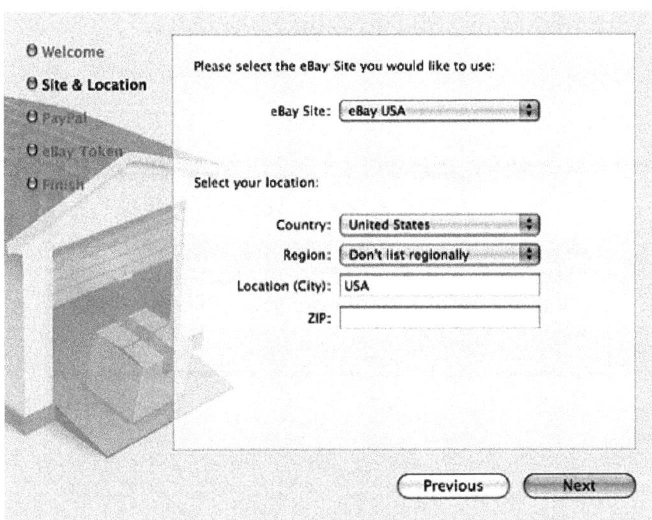

After providing the information click **Next**. In this section of the setup process you can specify whether you would like to accept PayPal as one of the default payment methods for your auctions posted with GarageSale.

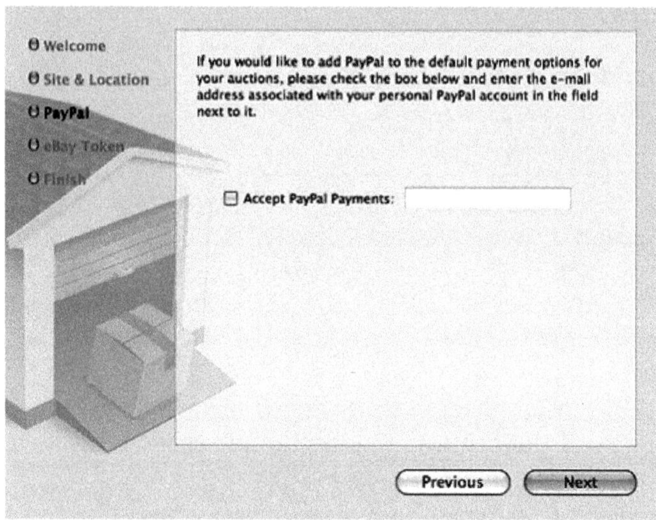

After completing this information click *Next* to get your *eBay token.*

Disable the *I will authorize GarageSale later* checkbox if you want to authorize your eBay account right away.

The Access Token

GarageSale requires an *access token* to connect to the eBay system. This is a secret code GarageSale needs to help keep your account secure.

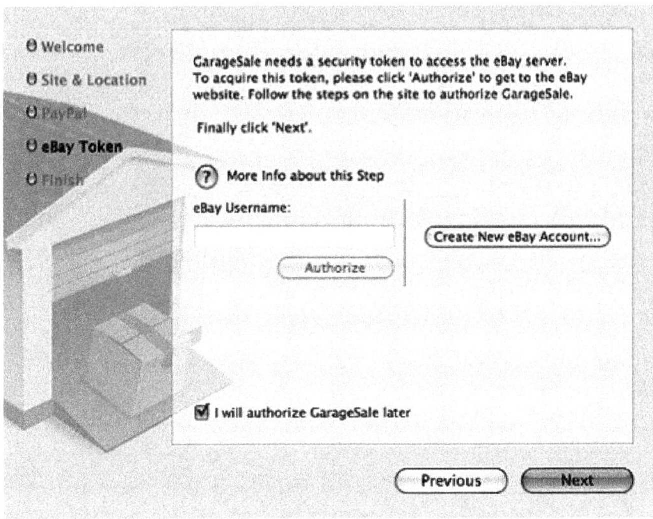

See the following section, *Authorizing Garagesale To Use Your Ebay Account,* for details about *tokens.* Make sure you are using the same eBay account information for both parts of the registration! After completing the process, switch back to the GarageSale installation window and press *Next.*

eBay maintains a databank of category information. To make working with categories faster, GarageSale stores this information locally. Depending on which eBay site you choose, the category information could amount to ten to fifteen megabytes of data that must downloaded before you can use GarageSale. This is of special interest to users with a dial-up or other slow internet connection. Be aware that clicking on *Finish* will begin downloading the category data.

Authorizing GarageSale To Use Your Ebay Account

GarageSale requires an *access token* to connect to the eBay system. This is a secret code GarageSale needs to help keep your account secure.

An *access token* grants a single application access to your eBay account, in this case GarageSale. eBay requires an authorized client applications or services to use a token. This token is used as a safer alternative to saving your eBay username and password locally on your hard drive.

GarageSale needs a token to perform its operations such as adding auctions, getting auction categories, etc. with your eBay account. After filling in your eBay username and clicking the *Authorize* button, GarageSale will automatically point your web browser to the eBay token web page. Follow the instructions on the web page to authorize GarageSale. Then return to GarageSale and click *Next*.

GarageSale will retrieve your access token from eBay. This token will only be saved in your personal keychain. You can view and delete it using the keychain access application in the utilities directory located in your *applications folder*.

If you leave *I will authorize GarageSale later* checked, you can go to GarageSale Preferences —> Accounts and press *Add*. Type in your *eBay Username* and press *Authorize*. This will open an agreement on your browser for you to complete. Then go back to the preferences window and press the *Fetch Token* button. This will give you your eBay token and set up a new account which you can view in Preferences —> Accounts.

CHAPTER 2
Getting Started

Modes

When using GarageSale you work in one of two modes. You can identify your current mode by the active tab at the top of the main window.

Preview Mode Preview your auctions.

Editor Mode Edit your auctions.

Preview Mode

Preview Mode gives you an idea of how your auction will look after you have submitted it to eBay. Check your layout decisions with the preview function quickly and easily. You can modify the layout in this mode as well. Due to the dynamic nature of eBay pages, some differences between the GarageSale preview and the actual auction may occur.

Since GarageSale version 4 you can edit your description and make your settings directly in Preview Mode!

Editor Mode

Editor Mode gets you to the core of your template and enables you to see and edit its images and description in rather straightforward fashion. If you are a HTML geek, feel free to impress the world with your abilities but don't forget to leave the little HTML checkbox on the right unchecked. If you use plain text, check this box to ensure it gets translated into proper HTML.

Inspector Window

The Inspector allows you to quickly access and change the auction options (e.g. categories, starting bid, shipping options, etc.). To open it just click on the *Inspector* icon in GarageSale's toolbar:

CHAPTER 3
General Usage

The Template Paradigm

Here are some hints on using GarageSale's template paradigm:

1. If you have information (disclaimer, etc) that should go into every auction, you can put just that information in special template and designate that template as master template in Preferences > New Template > Master template. Every time you create a new template all the information from the master template will be already there.

2. If you are frequently selling items from different categories (e.g. dolls), you can create a set of second level master templates that contain all your information specific to to a certain item category. Only fill in the information common to all items of a certain type. Use the *Duplicate* button before filling in any information for a specific item.

3. If you ever used a template to start an auction. Don't modify it. Use the *Duplicate* button instead. Chances are that you will have the same or a nearly identical in the future to sell. Also, when you modify the template that has a running auction, you will have a hard time revising that auction in case you find errors its description.

4. The template's are your true treasure. Therefore make sure to backup your Mac regularly. You would be surprised to know how often we get approached by users who lost thousands of templates when they didn't have a backup.

This template system is flexible enough to do what most people want. Remember to use the *Duplicate* button often. It's ok to have a set of partially filled in skeleton templates around.

GarageSale Icon Legend

Icons explained: Different colors and signs symbolize the state of your Auctions and Auction Templates. Take a look at the following legend for a more complete explanation:

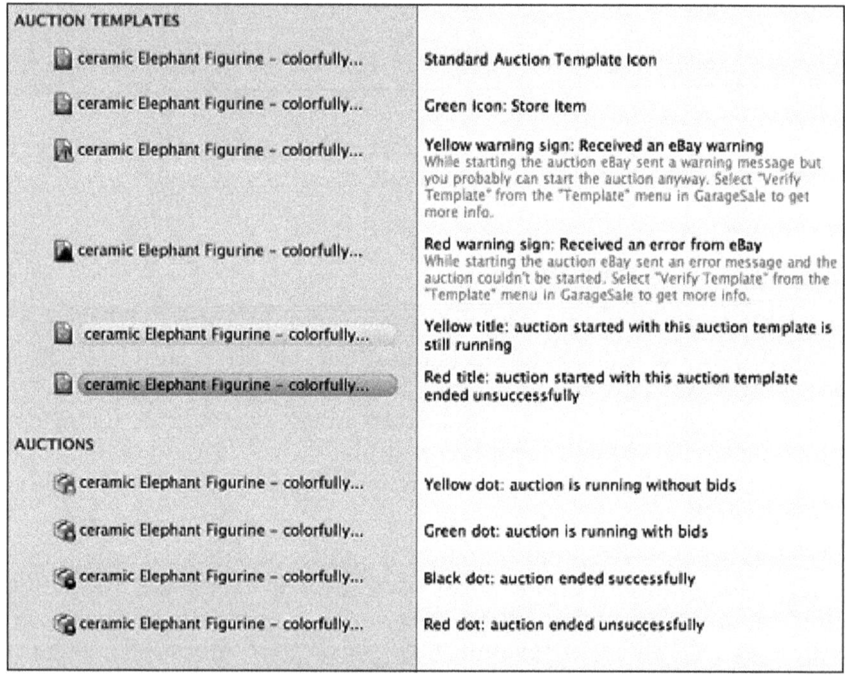

If you get a yellow warning sign when trying to start an auction eBay returned a warning about some aspect of your auction. You can choose to ignore it and still list your item. Select *Verify Template* from the *Template Menu* (see below) for details.

If you get a red warning sign: eBay refuses to list your item for a specific reason. Maybe verifying your templates will shed some light on it. If you don't get a helpful error message from eBay, try to list the exact same auction on the eBay webpage. Sometimes this will result in a more informative message than the one eBay provides third party applications like GarageSale.

Preparing your auction templates

CHAPTER 4
SETTING UP AUCTION TEMPLATES

When you first start up the program, a blank auction called *New Auction Template* is created. You can create a blank auction template at any time by pressing the *New Template* button in the toolbar. Auctions appear automatically in the templates list on the left-hand side of the GarageSale window.

To begin, we will lead you step-by-step through the process of filling in an auction template.

To create an auction, complete the following entries. Some entries are required for your auction. Other entries are optional and incur an additional cost with eBay. In the default configuration of GarageSale, items requiring additional cost are highlighted in red.

Editor Mode vs. Preview Mode

You have two possibilities in setting up your auction. In addition to the familiar *Editor Mode* in previous versions, *GarageSale 4.0* introduced the *Preview Mode* which allows you to modify the description directly inside the preview.

To choose the mode you prefer, click on the appropriate button in the middle of the bar. Here you see the preview mode.

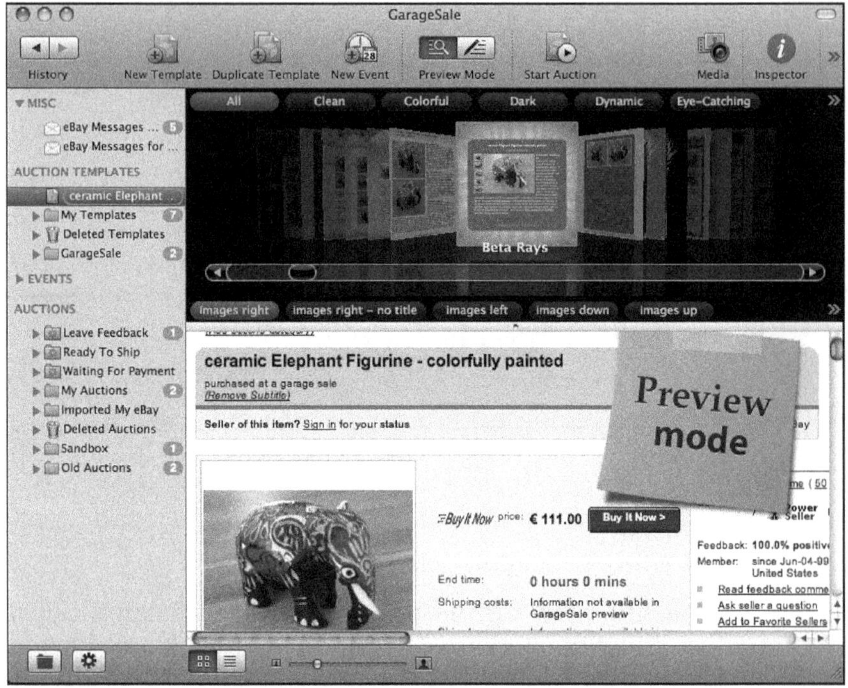

Item Description—Editor Mode

Subtitle

An optional title for your auction, providing more detail about your item *(additional ebay fee)*.

Images

You may include one image in the auction without additional fees if you are using eBay's Picture Service (EPS) for image storage (this is GarageSale's default setting). Additional images stored on EPS imply extra charges.

You may use a Web server (via FTP or WebDAV) for auction image storage, or you may upload images to your MobileMe account. You can set up the necessary configuration for your server in the Preferences window. If you are planning to use MobileMe, make sure you have entered your MobileMe account details. If you want to use a Web server via FTP, you will need to enter your user ID and password in GarageSale's setup pane, along with the exact path to your image storage directory on the server. You will also enter the HTTP URL path to that directory, which will allow GarageSale to perform a test upload and then display the test image in your browser as confirmation that the FTP path is correct.

GarageSale allows you to import auction images directly from iPhoto, from your digital camera, from your iSight camera or from image files on your Mac. If you already have images uploaded to your Web server, GarageSale can include these in your auction template by referencing the URL for these images. Use the '+' button below the image table to add images from one of these sources.

A picture may be chosen as the gallery image. This image will appear in the eBay category listing next to your item when the *All Items including Gallery Preview* tab is chosen by a customer. Use the button with the stylized image frame on the left to mark an image as gallery image. You can also simply drag and drop the chosen picture into the gallery image area to the right:

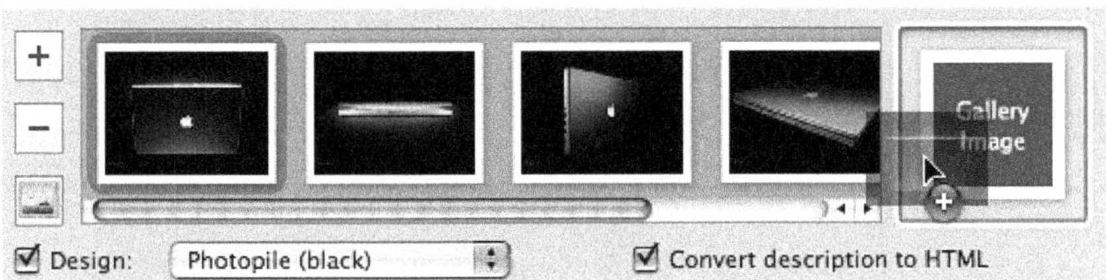

Image Drop Zone

In the *Preview Mode* you will always find a drop zone inside the templates. You can easily drag and drop the images you want to add to your auction.

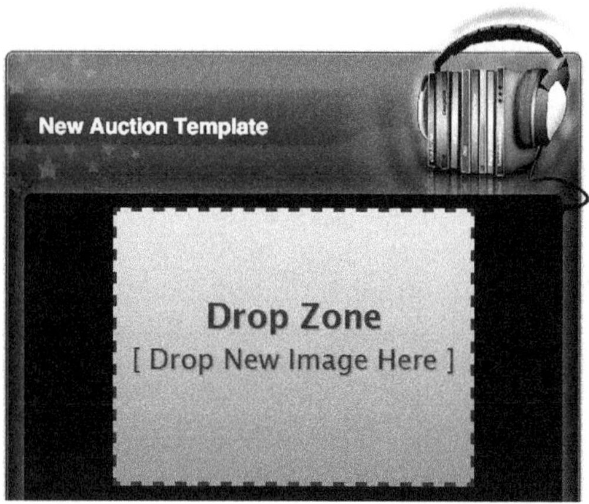

Media Browser

While in preview mode, you can open the Media Browser and select the pictures to drop into the drop zone.

You can browse your computer, directly in iPhoto or simply inside GarageSale.

> **Importing Photos**
>
> GarageSale allows you to import auction images directly from iPhoto, from your digital camera, from your iSight camera or from image files on your Mac.

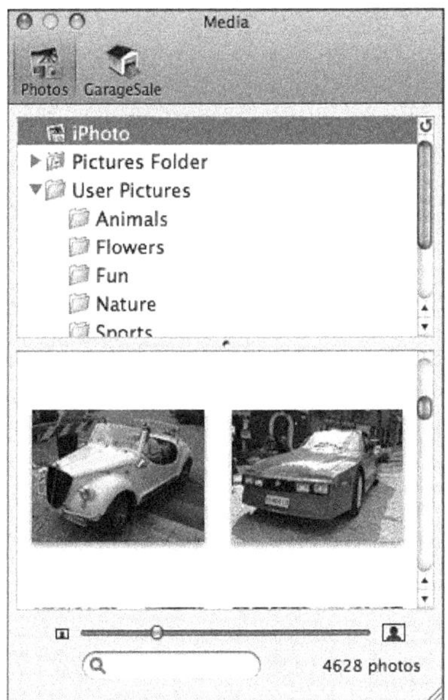

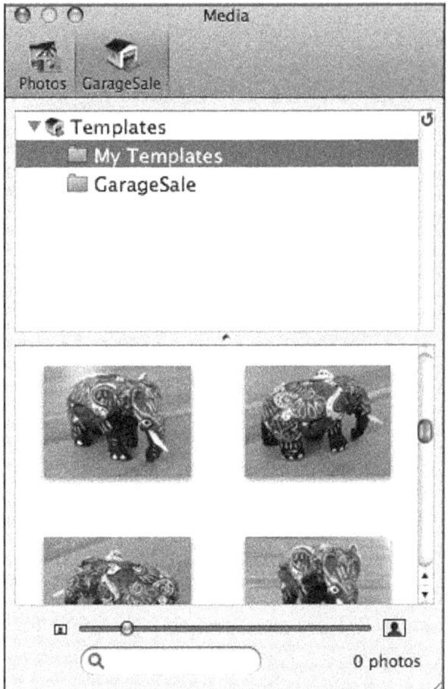

If you are adding pictures to your iPhoto library while GarageSale is running, click the little refresh arrow for the Media Browser to refresh.

Description

Enter your product's description in the text field below the image area.

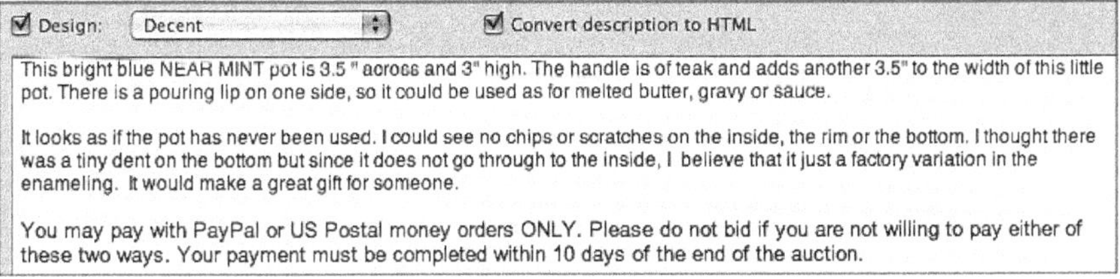

For example:

> This wonderful piece of railroad history is called The Santa Fe Magazine The Railway Exchange, Chicago Volume XXIII November 1929 Number 12. It is in good condition considering its age, and full of wonderful advertising from the era. There are 160 pages of great information with arti-

cles on everything about Los Angeles just before the Great Depression. This would be a great gift for the collector of railroad memorabilia...

You can then format your item description in two ways:

1. By default, enter your description in text form, controlling the formatting with the standard Mac OS font menu items, such as **bold** or *italic*. When using this method, be sure the checkbox convert description to HTML is checked.

2. You may also enter your description as HTML tagged text. In this case, make sure that the checkbox *Convert Description to HTML* is **NOT checked**. No further conversion is required for HTML.

[*GarageSale 3* only: Clicking on the pencil icon in the toolbar the text field opens a separate editing window. Edit your text in the top pane of the window. Preview your description text in the lower pane.]

Listing Design

GarageSale can also apply a listing design to your item's description:

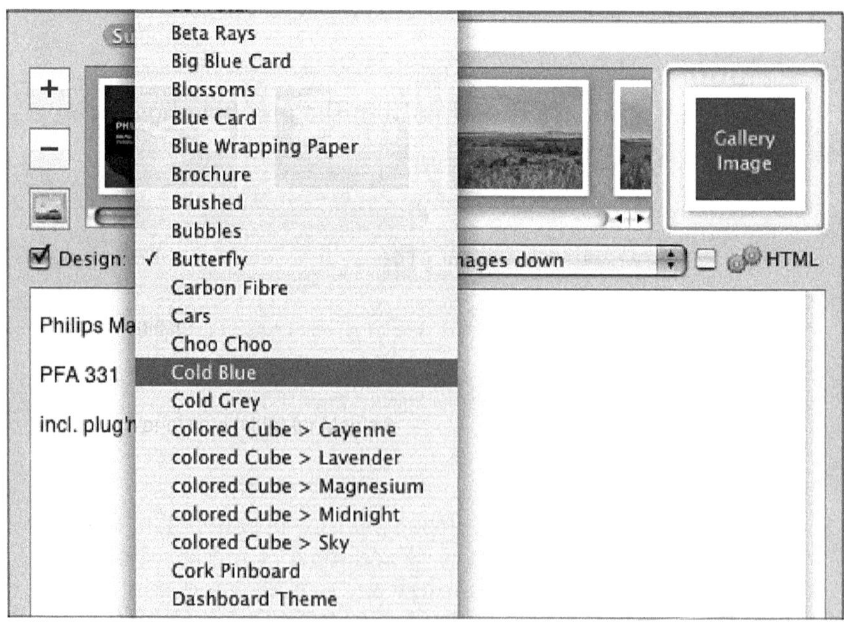

You can also pick a Listing Design through the *Choose Listing Design* command in the *Template Menu*:

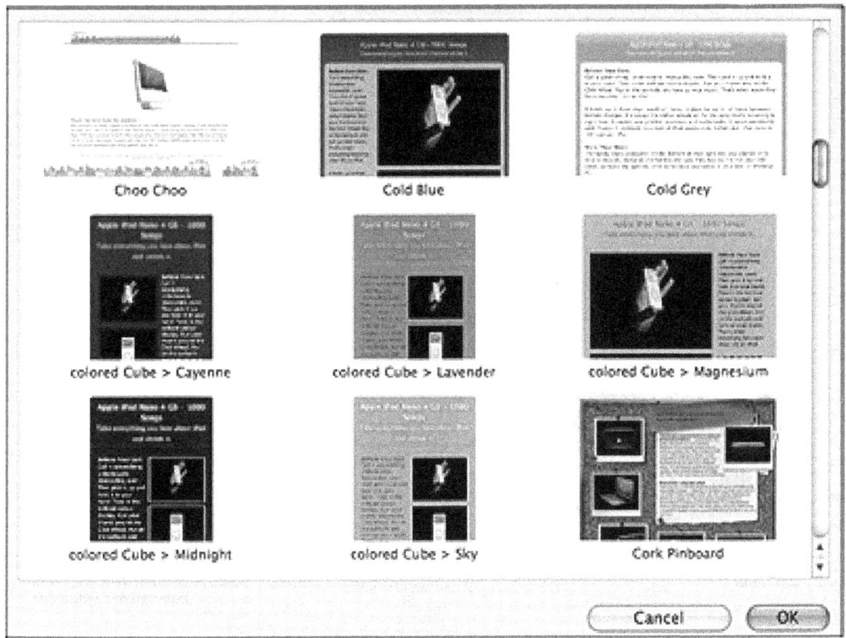

Use the *Preview Mode* to get an idea on how your auction would look when using a certain design. While in *Preview Mode*, use the Listing Design command's submenu in the *Template Menu* to cycle through the available designs.

See the section *Creating Own Listing Design Templates* for a guide on how to create new listings or customize existing ones.

Layout

In addition to the numerous listing designs you can modify the layout, i.e. you can choose the arrangement of the pictures and the auction text. Within seconds you can easily modify the layout of your auction.

Here are examples of five different picture layouts:

You may include one image in the auction without additional fees if you are using eBay's Picture Service (EPS) for image storage (this is GarageSale's default setting). Additional images stored on EPS imply extra charges.

You may use a Web server (via FTP or WebDAV) for auction image storage, or you may upload images to your .Mac account. You can set up the necessary configuration for your server in the Preferences window. If you are planning to use .Mac, make sure you have entered your .Mac

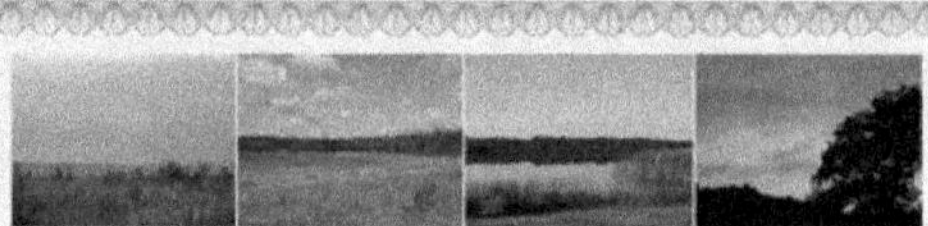

You may include one image in the auction without additional fees if you are using eBay's Picture Service (EPS) for image storage (this is GarageSale's default setting). Additional images stored on EPS imply extra charges.

You may use a Web server (via FTP or WebDAV) for auction image storage, or you may upload images to your .Mac account. You can set up the necessary configuration for your server in the Preferences window. If you are planning to use .Mac, make sure you have entered your .Mac account details. If you want to use a Web server via FTP, you will need to enter your user ID and password in GarageSale's setup pane, along with the exact path to your image storage directory on the server. You will also enter the HTTP URL path to that directory, which will allow GarageSale to perform a test upload and then display the test image in your browser as confirmation that the FTP path is correct.

GarageSale allows you to import auction images directly from iPhoto, from your digital camera, from your iSight camera or from image files on

You may include one image in the auction without additional fees if you are using eBay's Picture Service (EPS) for image storage (this is GarageSale's default setting). Additional images stored on EPS imply extra charges.

You may use a Web server (via FTP or WebDAV) for auction image storage, or you may upload images to your .Mac account. You can set up the necessary configuration for your server in the Preferences window. If you are planning to use .Mac, make sure you have entered your .Mac account details. If you want to use a Web server via FTP, you will need to enter your user ID and password in GarageSale's setup pane, along with the exact path to

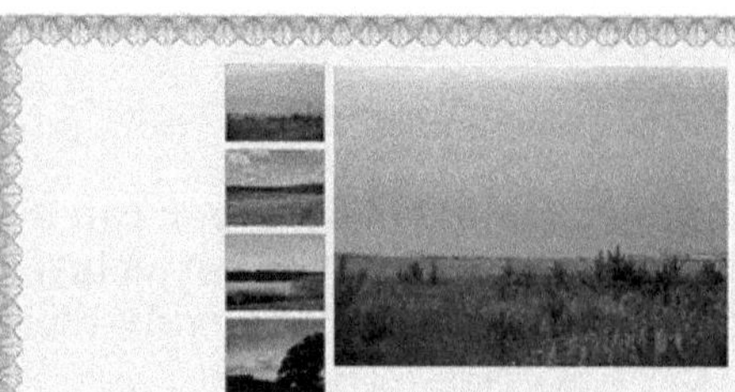

You may include one image in the auction without additional fees if you are using eBay's Picture Service (EPS) for image storage (this is GarageSale's default setting). Additional images stored on EPS imply extra charges.

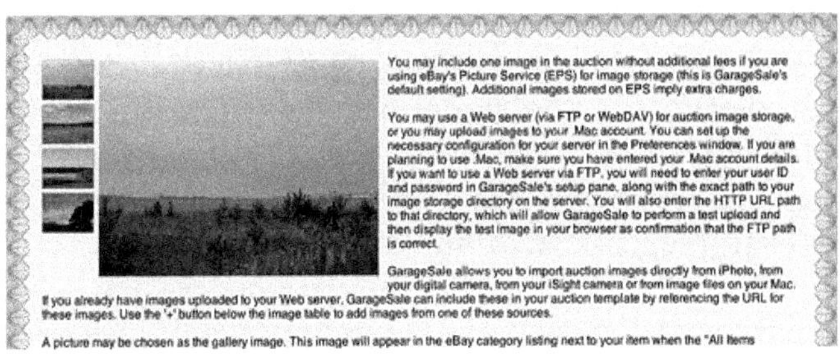

The last two layouts above contain a *hover gallery*. When the user passes his cursor over a small picture—a larger one appears.

The most convenient way to decide about the layout is to check out the possibilities in the *Preview Mod*. Simply *control-click* on the chosen design *(on the right)* or somewhere within the html-view *(on the left)*:

As you can see, there are 3 images on top *(as selected)*. You could, for example, choose *thumbnail images right*...

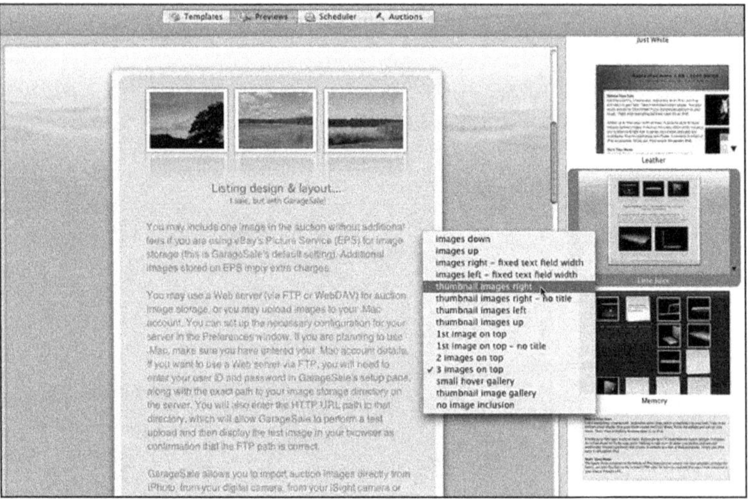

...and you can instantly see the new layout:

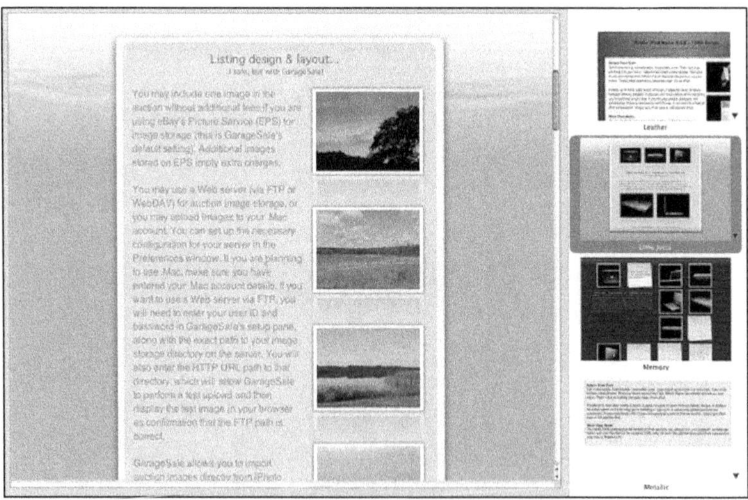

This new layout option gives you **1155 different design possibilities** for a single auction!

Remember, with GarageSale's Free Picture Service it is all **for free** (for up to 10 pictures per listing)!!! And you do not need any configuration like FTP etc. Simply select and enjoy.

CoverFlow for Auction Designs

GarageSale 3.2 offers you, with CoverFlow, a new convenient way to choose your listing design. You simply select the designs category at the top of the CoverFlow window

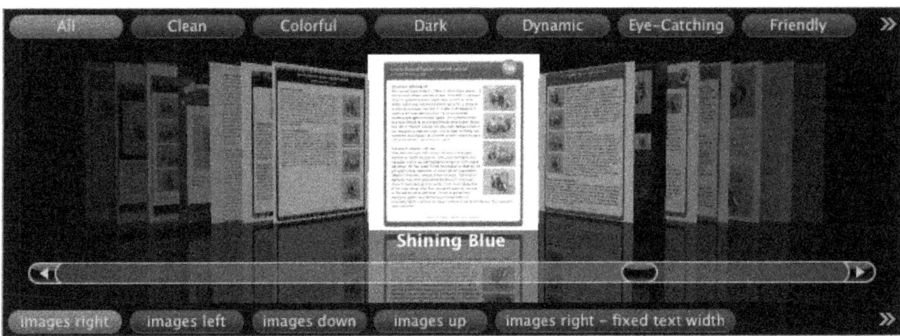

You can limit your choice by activating the bottoms of certain design category (one or more). You will then only see the chosen selection. To see all design possibilities select *all*.

Then at the bottom of the CoverFlow window, choose the appropriate layout. By selecting a layout you can, for example, decide on where to place the images within the chosen design.

You can immediately check out the result in the preview window and start your auction right away.

Auction Options

In *GarageSale 4.0* the distinct modes for auctions and templates have been unified into a single view where each item is accessible with a single click. In addition, the new *Inspector* makes life even easier.

Inspector

The new *Inspector* allows you to quickly access and change the auction options.

The remaining auction options—regardless of the GarageSale version, and whether or not you are using the Inspector—have been split in three sections. In older versions, you can use the switch control at the lower right of the window to switch between these sections. Within the Inspector, click on the buttons at the top.

The basic auction options themselves remain the same, no matter which version you are using. However, to profit from all options—such as those for Skype or charity donations—and to set up your auction as carefully as possible, you should use the latest version. *GarageSale 4*, for example, is the most extensive update in GarageSale history, with crucial modifications.

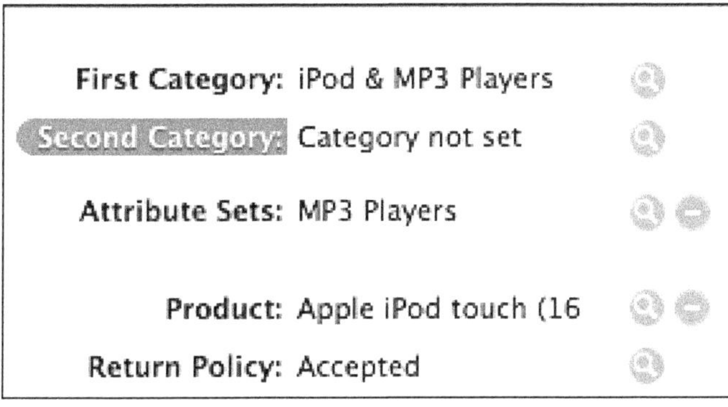

First Category, Second Category

eBay provides a large number of categories to make your item easier to find. Click the *magnifying glass* button to select a category. *(required)*

Optionally, list your item in more than one category to make it more visible *(additional category fee)*. Listing in more than one category may result in double fees for other options, (e.g. bold title or highlighted title.)

Attribute Sets

Many categories on eBay offer so-called item attribute sets. These are an optional and free-of-charge opportunity to further describe your item in a standardized way, thus making them easier to find for potential buyers. Click magnifying glass to specify attributes for your item. See the *Item Attributes* section for more information.

Border, Bold, Highlighted Title, Gallery, (Homepage) Featured

You can choose several enhancements for your auction:

The options will make your auction's title appear in bold or highlighted in the eBay category listing or search result. You can also add a border or the featured gallery effect *(additional fees)*.

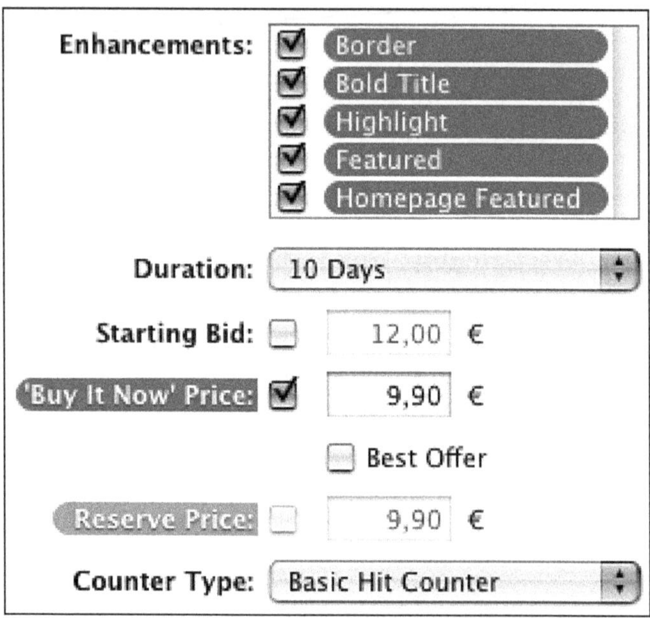

Duration

Set the duration of your auction. eBay provides standard auctions lengths that you can choose here. The contents of this popup menu might change if you have configured GarageSale to upload your auction to your eBay store.

Starting Bid and Buy It Now Price

Choose at least one of these entries. If you plan to offer a fixed-price auction, use *Buy It Now* only. If you only want a bidding auction, choose *Starting Bid*.

Buy It Now Price: The price at which you are willing to sell your item immediately. If you don't select a *starting bid* for your auction, the auction will be a *fixed price auction (different listing fee)*.

Starting Bid: This is the starting bid at which you would like to offer your item. Remember: it is always possible that you will have to sell your item for this price. So choose wisely!

Best Offer

This auction is only available on selected eBay sites and in certain categories, and only if you are starting your auction as a fixed price auction (no starting bid, only 'buy it now'). With this option enabled potential buyers can ask you whether you are willing to sell your item at a lower price than the given fixed price.

Reserve Price

The reserve price is not available for all eBay sites. This is the price below which you do not want to sell the item. Your reserve price will not be shown on eBay, but the fact that there is a reserve price is visible to bidders *(additional fee)*.

Counter Type

Select the desired access counter type for your auction.

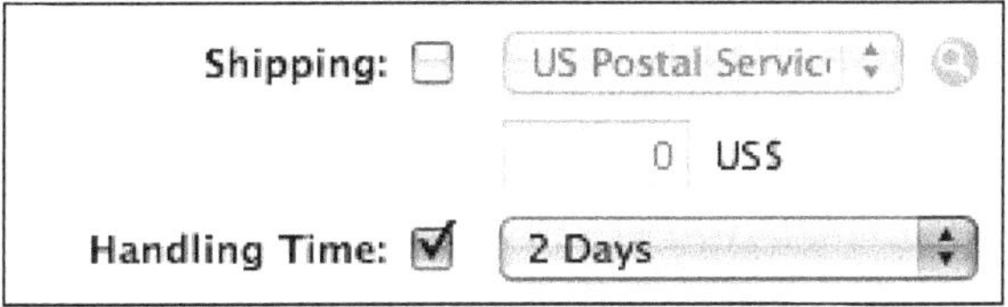

Shipping

Specify what shipping services you offer here. If you want to offer more than a single shipping service for your buyers to choose from, click the magnifying glass to see the options. For more information on how to specify several domestic and international shipping services see *Shipping Options*. Be aware that the names of the actual options you choose (UPS Ground, UPS 2nd Day Air, etc.) might not show up in the Preview of your template. You might see only the prices you entered for the services. The names of the services *will* appear, however, in your eBay listing. Don't worry. This minor aberration in the Preview is a deliberate safeguard to prevent GarageSale from stumbling over many frequent changes eBay makes in this portion of its interface.

Payment Options & Instructions

Options: Choose the payment methods you are willing to accept by clicking on the magnifying glass. This will present you with a list of available payment methods.

Instructions: Payment to be made within 10 days of auction close. I accept Paypal, checks or money orders (need to clear bank before shipment). Destinations outside USA will require different shipping cost.

Deposit Settings for eBay Motors US

When selling cars or trucks on eBay Motors US, sellers can specify their deposit settings in this section:

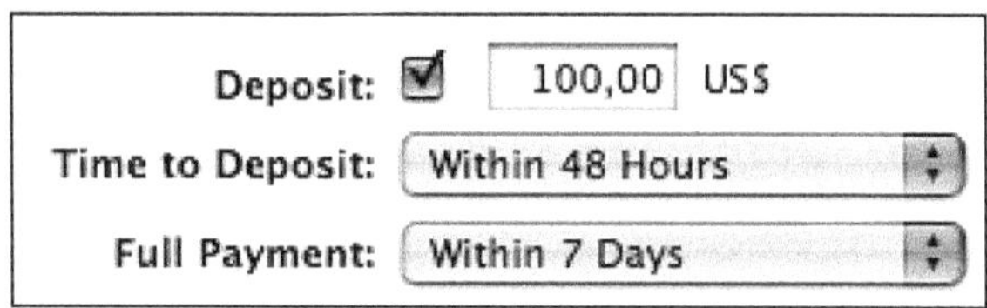

Deposit: The required deposit amount.

Time to Deposit: The period of time your are expecting the buyer to send you the deposit.

Full Payment: The period of time your are expecting the buyer to send you remaining amount.

Advanced Auction Options

Additional auction properties can be specified in the Advanced section.

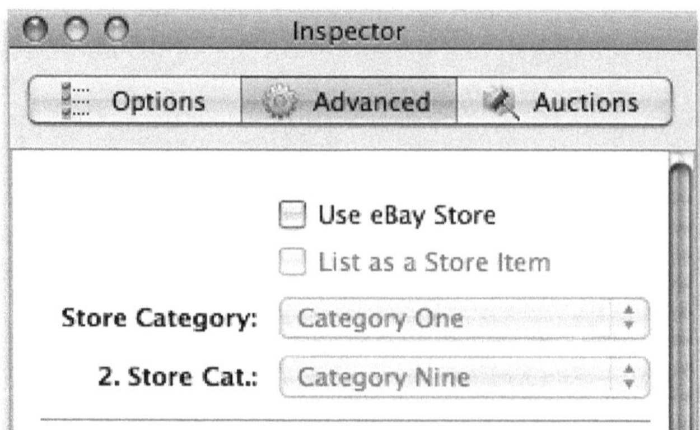

Use eBay Store

If this checkbox is enabled, GarageSale will associate your listing with your eBay store. The item will show up in your eBay Store as well in the regular eBay categories you selected. You have to be an eBay store owner at eBay to use this option. Please go to the *Preferences* panel and download the list of your store categories before using this option.

List as a Store Item

This checkbox is only available when you enabled the above option Use eBay Store. If you activate this setting, the item will be listed as a store item. It will only appear in your store, not in the regular categories. eBay also allows longer durations for store items and the listing fee for store items is greatly reduced compared to regular listed items.

Store Category & 2nd Store Category

eBay allows you to create custom categories in your store. Once you downloaded the list of your custom categories in the Categories section of the GarageSale Preferences window you can choose two categories for your item to appear in.

Quantity

If you want to auction several items of the same kind all at once, enter the quantity of items in this box.

SKU

SKU stands for "stock keeping unit." It is a term for a unique numeric identifier, used mostly to refer to a specific product in inventory or in a catalog. If you are selling several items of the same kind you can in this way differentiate between them. This is rather useful for professional sellers.

EPS options

If you are using eBay's picture service (EPS) for image storage, you can choose between several options offered, e.g. supersize pictures (larger images) or picture pack. Selecting anything other than 'standard' implies additional charges.

Immediate payment

Immediate Payment is a free option that can be applied to listings with a Buy It Now offering, including auction-type listings and Stores items. By choosing this option, the seller requires immediate payment through PayPal before the listing can end. Once the payment is confirmed, the listing will officially end.

Buyer Requirements

The buyer requirement settings allow you, for example, to block eBay users who didn't register a PayPal account to bid on your item. In addition to the "Buyer needs PayPal requirement" with *GarageSale 5.2* and newer you can block buyers from countries you don't ship to and buyers with a record of unpaid item strikes. You can also select several templates at once and choose the corresponding menu item from the *Template Menu*.

Keep in mind that you are in this way possibly reducing the number of potential buyers.

Options? You want options?

GarageSale has1155 different design possibilities for each auction you create!

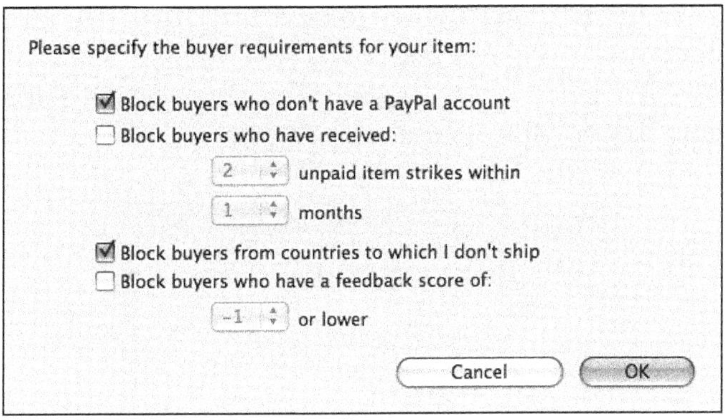

Please specify the buyer requirements for your item:

☑ Block buyers who don't have a PayPal account
☐ Block buyers who have received:
2 unpaid item strikes within
1 months
☑ Block buyers from countries to which I don't ship
☐ Block buyers who have a feedback score of:
-1 or lower

Cancel OK

Dispatch Time

The maximum number of business days it takes until the item is shipped to the winning bidder.

Get It Fast

If activated, your item will get marked with the 'get it fast' flag on eBay. This options is only available on certain eBay sites. It can only be enabled for buy it now items with a dispatch time of 1 day, for which at least one shipping option has been specified.

Now and New

An opportunity to sell your item *not only* the fixed price format but also indicating right from the start that your item is new and thus even more attractive. You give your buyers the convenience of a decent new product, which is certainly often appreciated! *(option not available in every country)*

Private Auction

This option hides the user IDs of bidders in the active public listing. IDs remain visible for the seller, though.

Keep in mind that on some eBay sites this is an extra fee option.

List as Classified Ads

With *GarageSale 5.2* and newer it is possible to list Classified Ads on eBay with GarageSale. This a a special format on eBay, where no actual bidding or purchasing takes place. Instead the seller pays a higher insertion fee for the presence of an ad in a certain category.

GarageSale right now supports the Classified Ad format on eBay.com, eBay.de, eBay.co.uk, and eBay.ie.

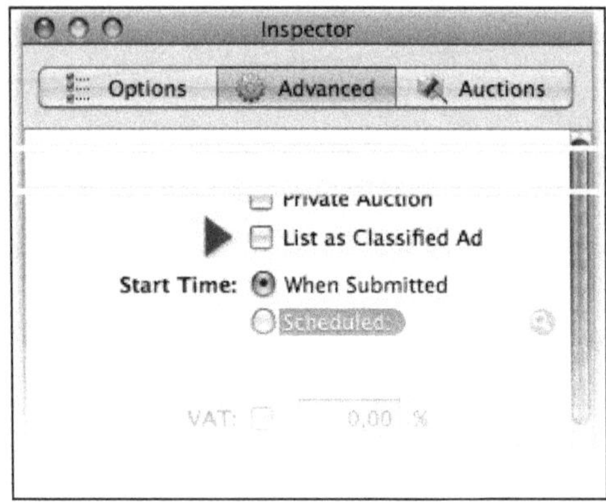

Auction Start Time

This feature allows you to use eBay's scheduling mechanism to schedule a starting time for your auction, beginning at any point in time after you have uploaded your auction information. *(at additional cost.)*

As of GarageSale version 2.1 you can use GarageSale's built-in Auction Scheduler to list items at a certain time without paying extra listing fees to eBay.

Sales tax

If you need to charge sales tax you can select a tax rate or enter a tax percentage in the Sales Tax section.

Skype

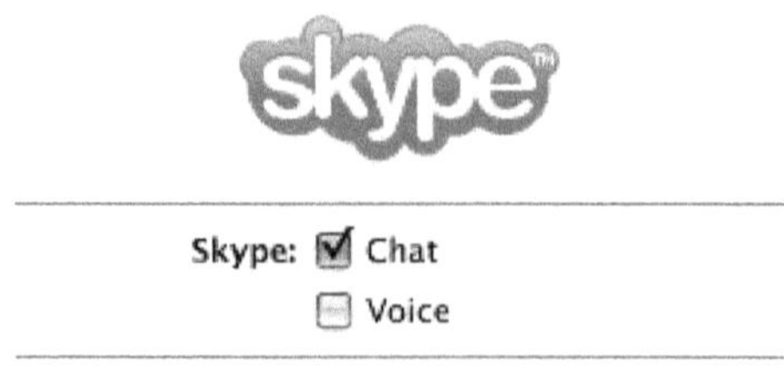

Sellers may have Skype buttons on their listings. Skype, an eBay company, is an application that you can install on your computer.

You can download and install Skype, and then use Skype to quickly chat with or call the seller with your questions.

Charity

eBay allows sellers to list items and collect proceeds (in whole or in part) on behalf of nonprofits either with eBay Giving Works (the dedicated program for charity listings on eBay) or without eBay Giving Works (as long as the listings meet specific guidelines for charitable solicitations).

First, you have to download available charity organizations:

You can then choose the organization and specify the percentage you are willing to donate.

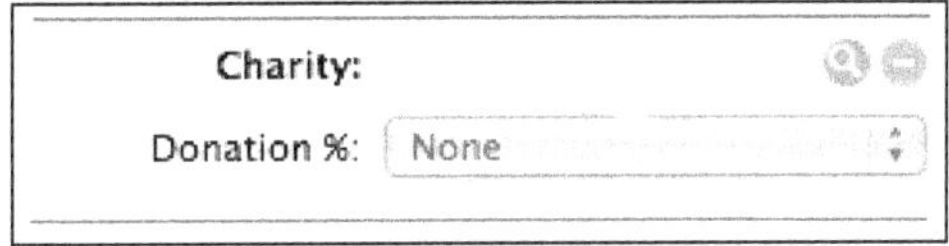

Site Information

eBay Site: eBay USA

Country: United States

Region: Don't list regionally

Currency: US$

Location (City): Your City

ZIP: ☑

Private Comment:

This was set during the initial configuration of GarageSale and may be changed in the GarageSale *Preferences* panel.

Country, Region, Location (City)

Please enter the country and region where you are and the location of the item.

Currency

The currency used for your auction. Except for eBay Canada, there is only one currency option available. On eBay Canada items can be listed in either Canadian or US dollars.

ZIP

If you want to make your item available via the location based search on eBay's website, activate the checkbox and enter your ZIP code here.

Private Comment

You can enter a private note for your auction template in this text box. You can leave notes for yourself here and later use the Search box to find the auction template again.

CHAPTER 5
SHIPPING OPTIONS

If you are only offering a single, flat fee shipping service you can specify directly in the *Shipping* section of the inspector window. If you want to offer international or flat shipping or multiple shipping services you have to bring up the *Shipping Options* panel.

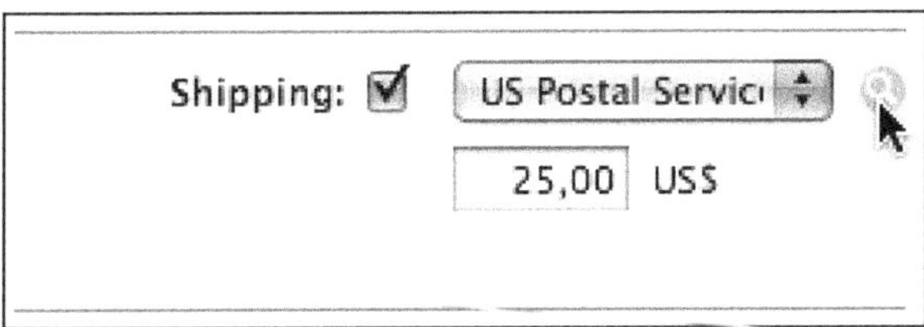

Working with the Shipping Options Panel

The shipping panel is split into three sections, one *general* section, one for *domestic* and one for *international* shipping options.

General

In the first one you can specify the *package info* (applies for calculated shipping only).

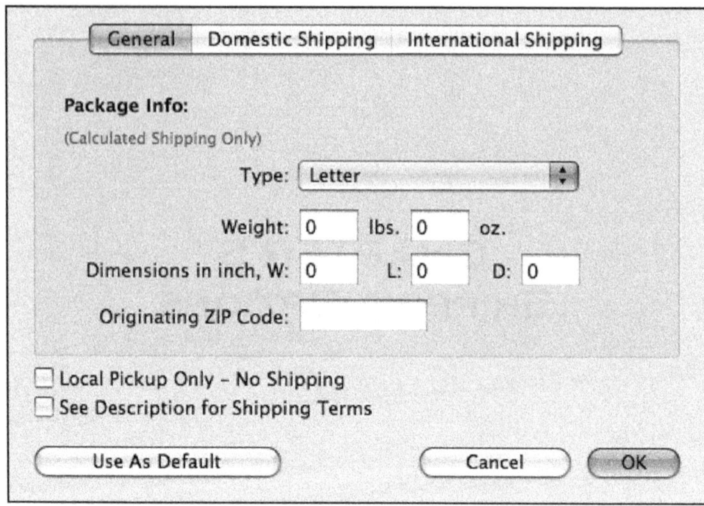

Domestic Shipping

In each of the latter sections you can specify up to *three different shipping services* and the *rates* at which you are willing to ship your item.

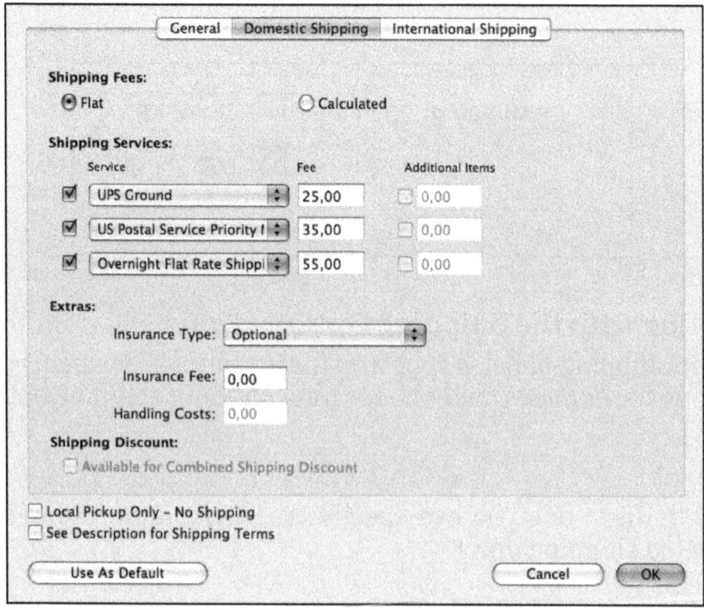

Local Pickup Only

If you are only offering your item for pickup by the buyer, select *Local Pickup Only—No Shipping.*

Special Shipping Terms

If you don't want to specify a shipping service and shipping fee for your item until your item has sold (or you would like to specify special shipping terms in the description text), activate the *See Descriptions for Shipping Terms* option.

Multiple quantity auctions

If you are starting a multiple item auction using the *quantity field*, you can also provide different shipping rates in the *Additional Items* field. If you do not provide an additional items shipping rate for multiple item auctions, eBay will assume that each additional item will add the basic shipping fee to the overall amount of the shipping.

Calculated Shipping

Calculated Shipping is only offered on the eBay USA and eBay Motors USA sites. The shipping options presented are drawn from the eBay site on which you are selling—not from the country where your items are located. There are two shipping categories for the services available, Domestic and International. For each category you may offer up to three shipping options, for example normal, express, etc. depending upon the eBay site you are using, there may also be additional options for Shipping Destinations, for example Europe, World-Wide, America, etc. Diverse criteria are cross-checked by GarageSale to simplify your choice of shipping options. At any given time only your available options are presented by the program.

International Shipping

In the International Shipping section you can select the parts of the world you are willing to ship your items to. You can also specify up to three international shipping services. If you want to offer one of those services for certain shipping destinations only, select the *Other Destinations* checkbox and choose those destinations from the *Destinations* pop-up menu.

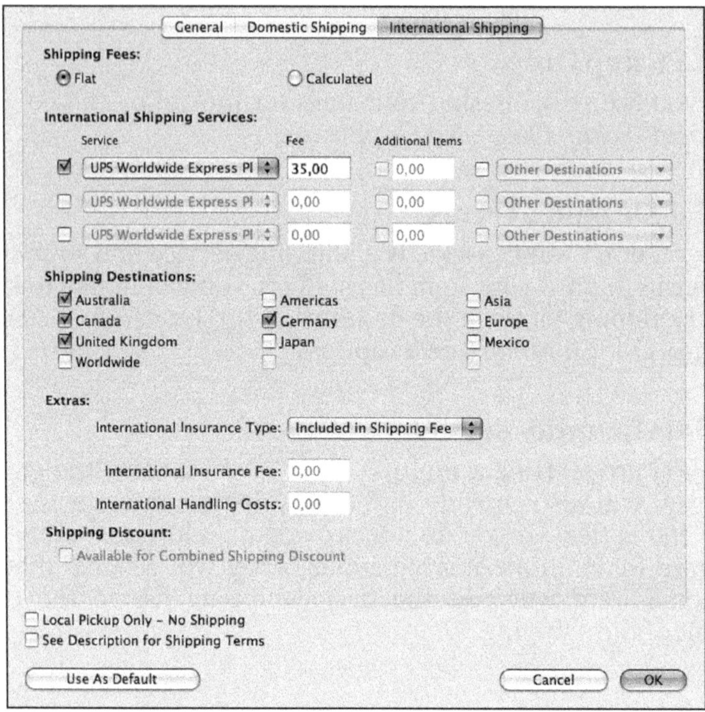

Insurance

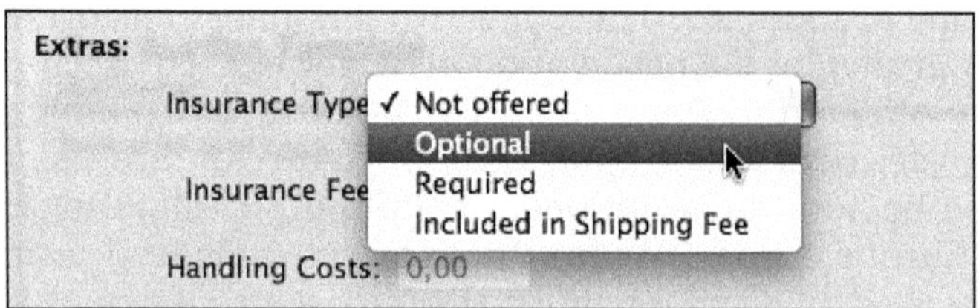

You can protect the package against loss or damage during shipping with insurance. It is up to you to decide whether insurance is included in the shipping fee, optional, required or maybe not offered at all. Here you specify the possibilities the buyer can choose from. Don't forget to enter the precise insurance fee and if necessary handling costs.

CHAPTER 6
GETTING AUCTION FEES

You can obtains the listing fees for a template by choosing *Get Listing Fees from eBay* from the *Template Menu*.

GarageSale will contact eBay...

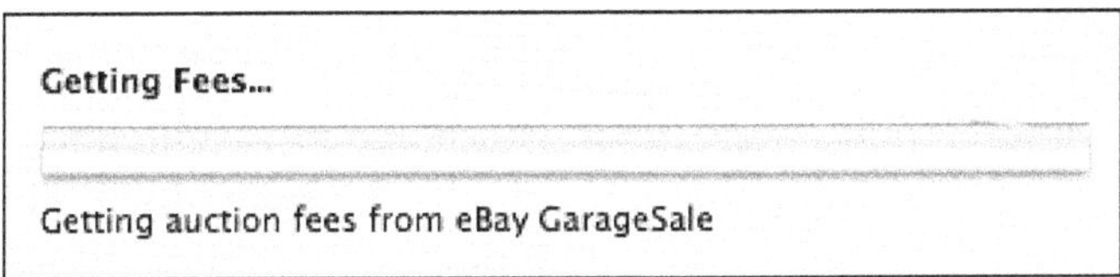

and open a panel displaying the fees you would be charged for listing the item(s).

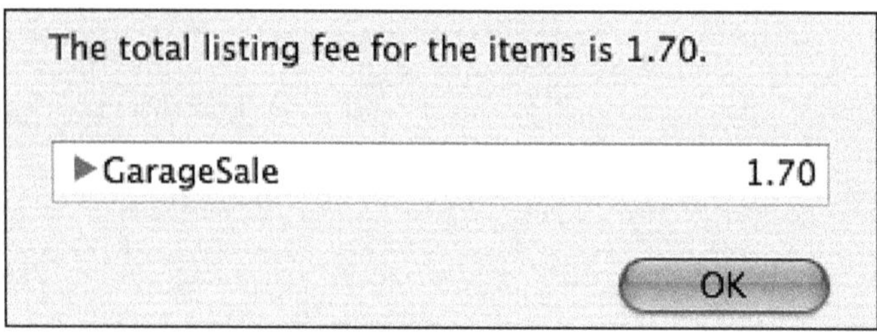

By the way, if you choose particularly expensive auction options GarageSale will warn you before starting your auction:

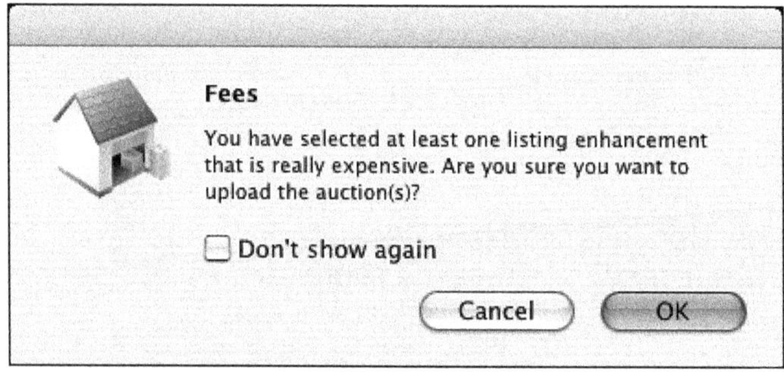

CHAPTER 7
LISTING WITH PRE-FILLED ITEM INFORMATION

eBay maintains a product catalogue for certain categories, like music CDs, DVDs or electronic gadgets. You can use GarageSale to associate your auction with a product listed in eBay's catalogue. When you start your auction eBay will automatically add a product description and a product image to your listing, freeing you from the task of collecting this information by yourself.

To **a**dd product information to your auction template, first select a catalogue-enabled category. Only if one of the selected categories is catalogue-enabled will the command *Get Product Information from eBay* in the *Template Menu* become available.

Choose this command to get to the *Catalog Search* panel.

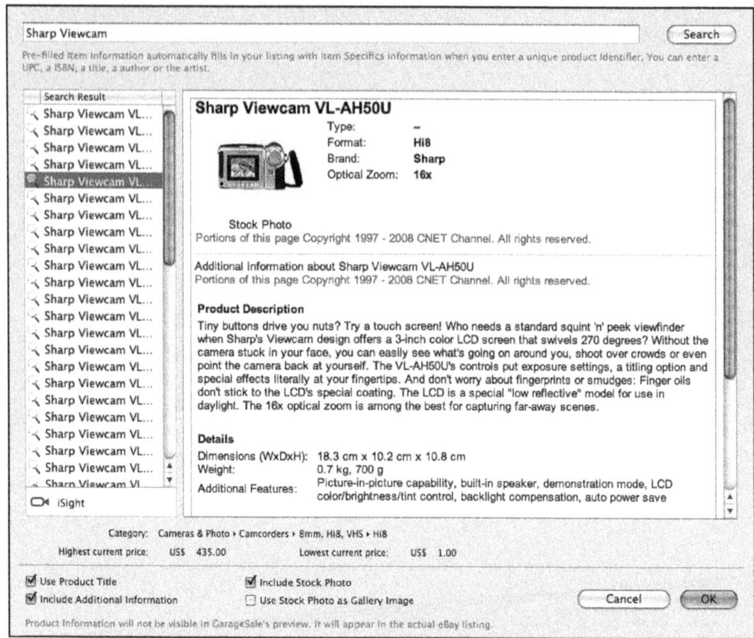

Use the search field at the top of the window to enter parts of the name, the UPC or the ISBN of the product you are looking for and press Search. After the search results are returned a list of products matching your search query will appear on the left side of the window. You can select items from this list to preview the information eBay will append to your item description. Note that a check mark appears next to the *List with eBay Product Information* menu item when you selected one of the products in eBay's catalogue. To remove the association between your auction template and a selected product choose the *List with eBay Product Information* item. The check mark will disappear to indicate that there's no product tied to your auction template.

CHAPTER 8
EDITING IMAGES

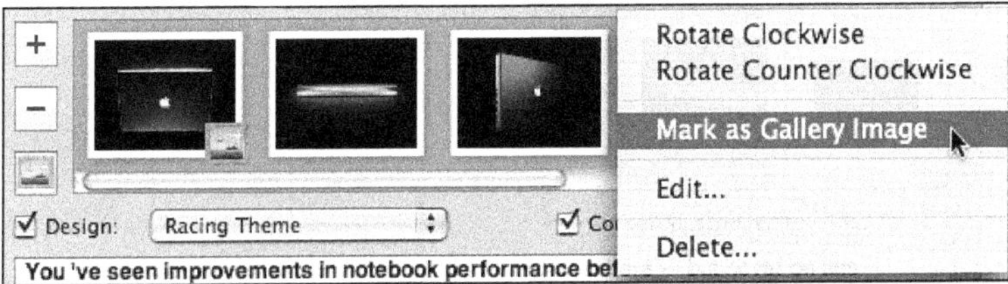

Rotating Images

You can rotate an image by clicking on it while you hold down the control key on your keyboard (if you have a two button mouse, right-click on an image). From the upcoming popup menu choose *Rotate Clockwise* or *Rotate Counter Clockwise*.

Gallery Image

Mark the image as Gallery Image. *Remember there is an additional fee.*

Editing Images

You can edit your images from within GarageSale by double-clicking an image or right-clicking and selecting *Edit*.

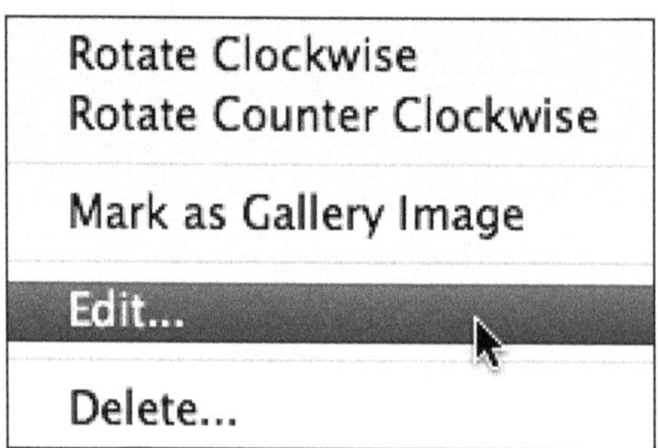

The window that appears will allow you to edit, apply different image filters or, crop your images before uploading them to eBay.

Please note that *the Image Editor is only available if you are using Mac OS X 10.4 or later.*

Here are some simple examples of what you can do:

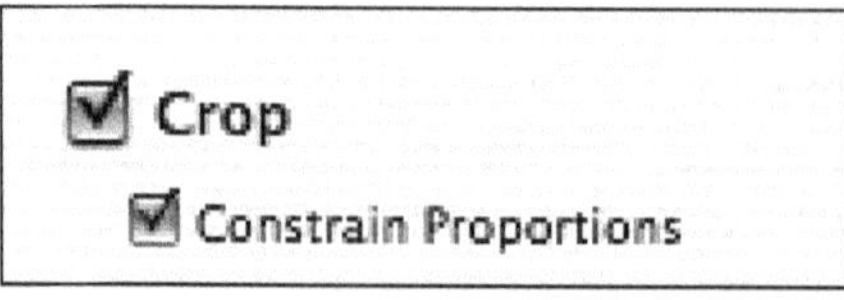

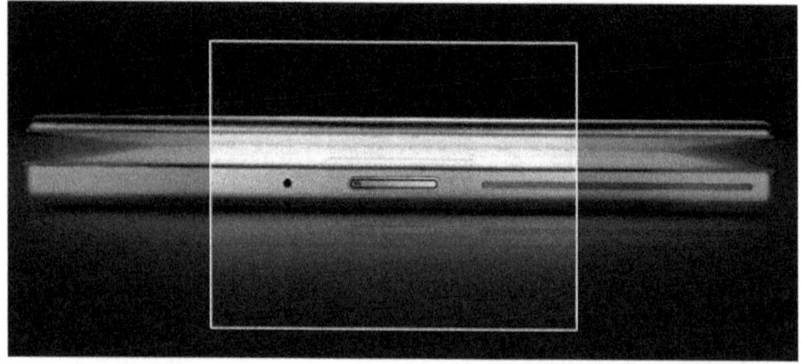

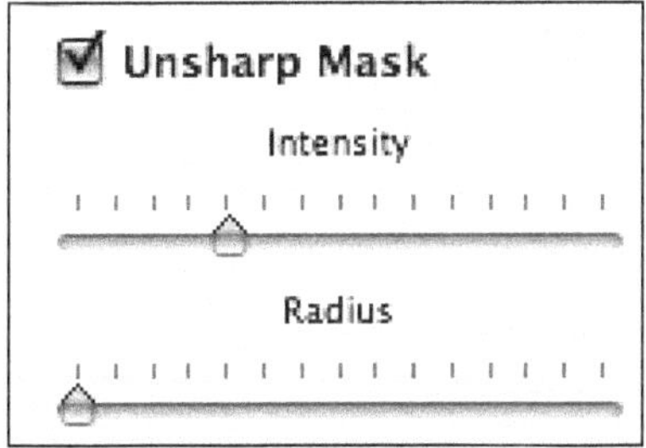
Unsharp Mask
Intensity
Radius

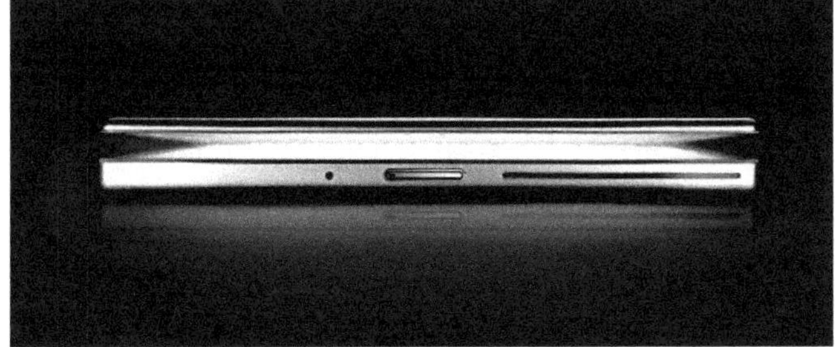

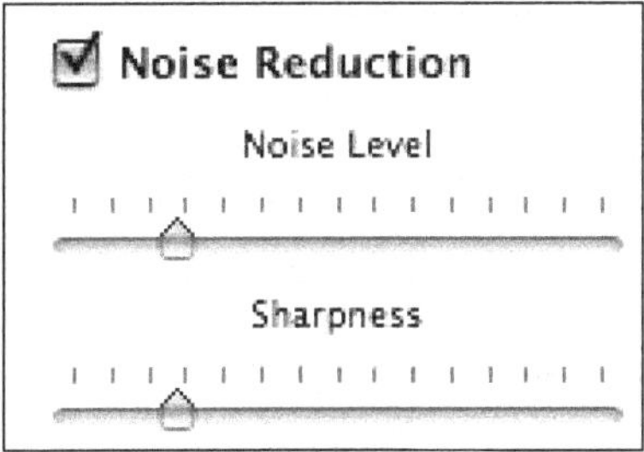
Noise Reduction
Noise Level
Sharpness

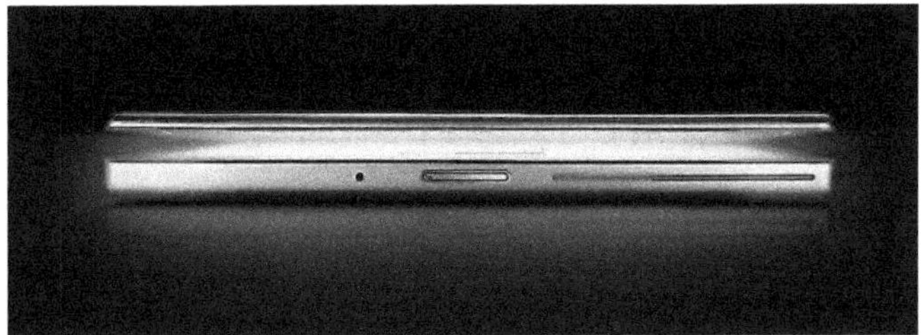

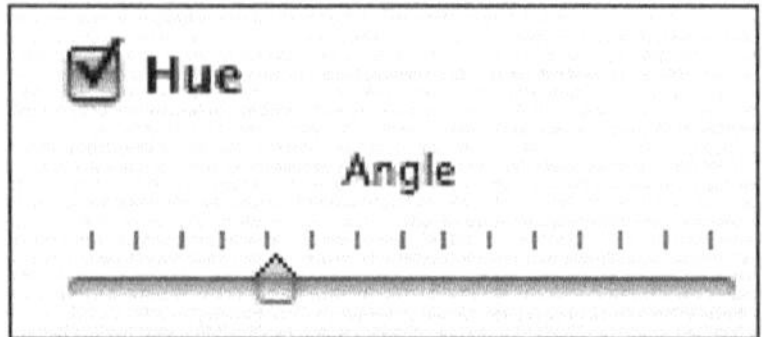
Hue
Angle

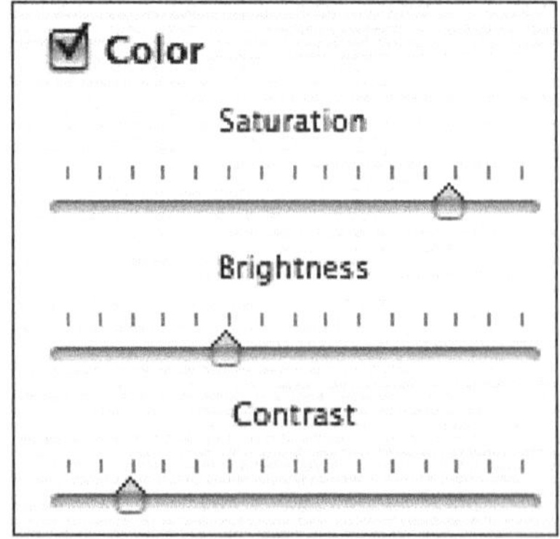
Color
Saturation
Brightness
Contrast

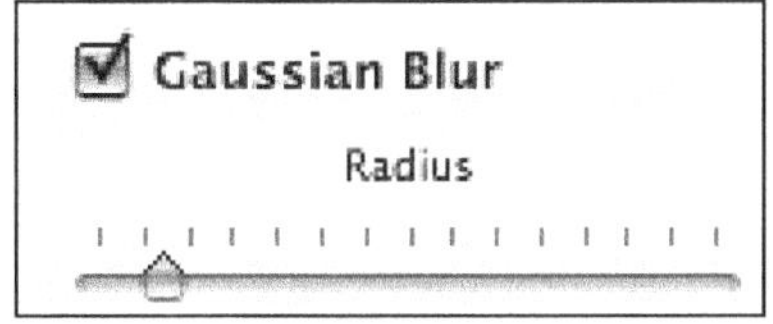

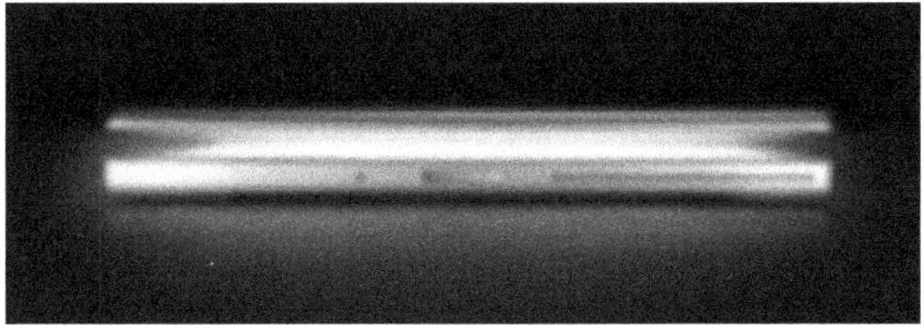

(But use this one with care. Remember that some buyers might prefer to actually see something.)

CHAPTER 9
SCHEDULING AUCTIONS

Starting auctions at a specified time gives you the opportunity to make them end when more users are on eBay, thus increasing the probability of gaining of high bids.

GarageSale supports two ways to make your auctions start at a certain point in time:

- eBay's Auction Scheduler
- GarageSale's built-in Auction Scheduler

The majority of GarageSale's users uses the built-in scheduler instead of eBay's scheduler, because it doesn't cost extra and allows scheduling of several auctions at once.

eBay's Auction Scheduler

You can use eBay's auction scheduler to schedule single auctions by setting the *auction start time* in an auction template's advanced options in the Inspector window. eBay will charge you an extra fee for using their scheduling feature.

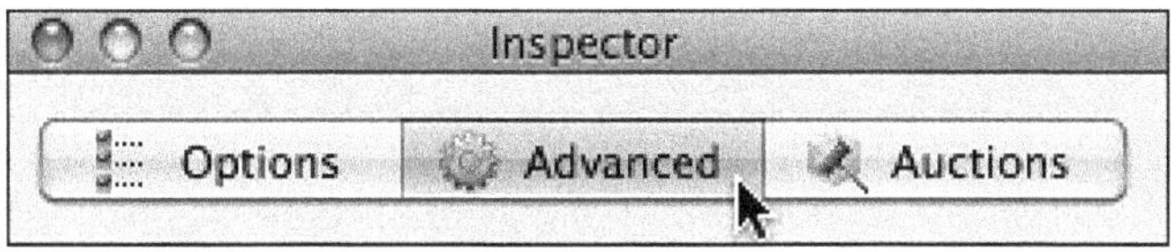

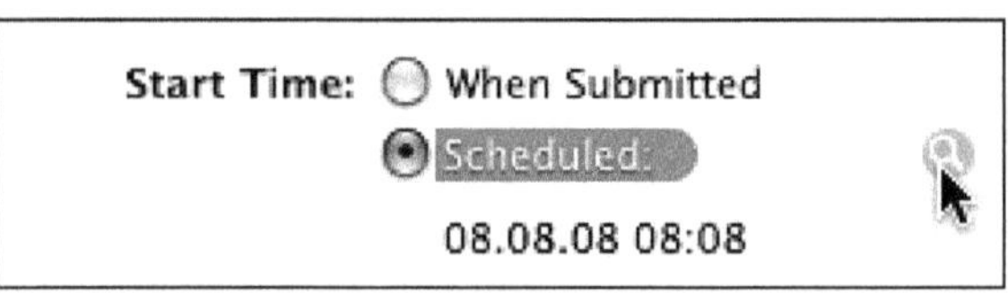

In the *Scheduling* panel, specify the date and time for your auction to start using your local time zone.

When eBay's scheduler is used, you need to use GarageSale's *Start Auction* command to upload your auction to eBay before your start date is reached. Once your auction is uploaded to eBay, you don't need to leave GarageSale running. eBay will make sure your auction is will start at the point in time you specified.

GarageSale's Built-in Auction Scheduler

GarageSale's built-in scheduling feature gives you the opportunity to schedule several auctions to start at a specific time without having to pay any additional fees. Optionally, you can put a time gap between auctions in order to give a winning bidder enough time to bid on your second auction, too.

Create new scheduler events

To make an auction start at a certain point in time, you need to create a new scheduling event in GarageSale. To do so, select the auction templates you want start at the same time and hit the *New*

Event button in the main window's toolbar. You can select several auction templates at once by holding down the shift key on your keyboard while selecting templates on the left-hand site outline view.

GarageSale will create a new event containing the templates you selected visible in the left-hand outline view's event section. The event's name is set to the first auction's title associated with it.

Initially every new event is not scheduled. As long as the event is not scheduled, you can make changes to its date and the templates its going to start.

Modifying events

After you create a new event you have to set its time. You can do so by bringing up to Inspector window with event selected.

> **The Scheduler**
>
> You might want to consider using GarageSale's built-in scheduler as your default. Unlike eBay's version, it doesn't cost extra and allows you to schedule several auctions at once.

Use the *date and time controls* to specify when GarageSale should start uploading your auctions for the selected event. Date and time are displayed **in the local time** of your system, **not** in the eBay time zone.

Enter the number of minutes you want to let pass in between auction starts in the *Interval field.* Leave this field to zero if you want the second auction to start as soon as the first one has finished uploading.

If you want to start the auctions using a certain eBay account, select it from the *Accounts* popup menu. Leave that field to the setting *Default account* if you only have one eBay account or want to use the account marked as default in GarageSale's *Preferences.*

Drag templates from left-hand templates list to the list of templates associated with the selected event at the window's right part.

Note, while working with the inspector, simply selected the template you would like to work with (without closing the inspector). The inspector will load the information automatically.

Scheduling Events

Once you specified all the settings for your event, click the *Enable Event* button to add your event to the list of scheduled events. When you do so, a panel will appear asking you whether or not you want to verify the selected templates with eBay before uploading.

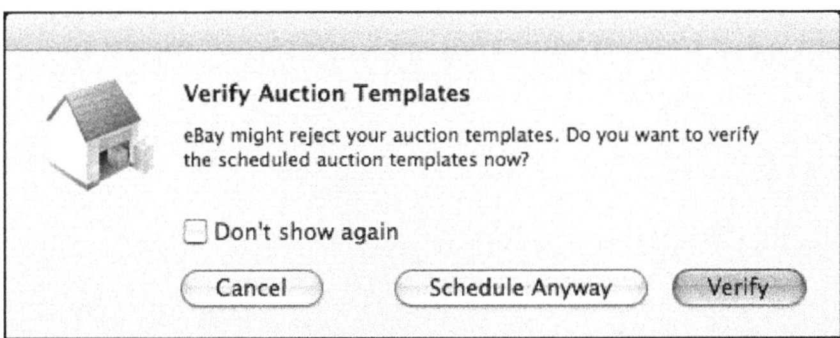

Verifying your event templates makes sure that eBay won't reject your auctions once they are automatically uploaded.

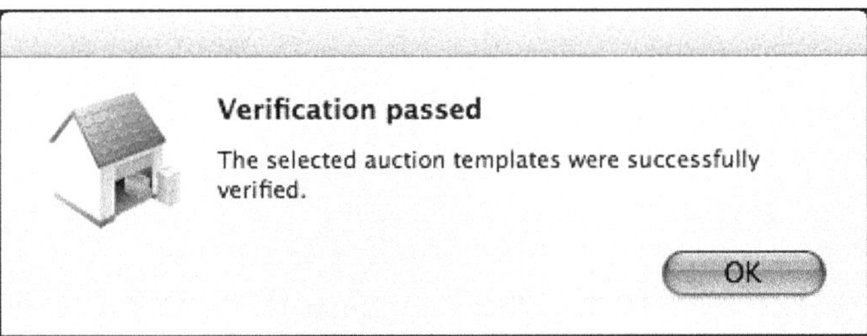

Remember to keep GarageSale running so it can upload your auctions at the right time!

(You might find the tutorial video *Scheduling Auctions* helpful in understanding this area.)

CHAPTER 10
EBAY STORES

You will also need to download the names of the categories you created in your eBay store to select them in GarageSale. Head to the *Accounts* section of the GarageSale *Preferences* panel, select your eBay account , and click *Update Now* in the eBay Stores section. GarageSale will download the store categories for the account that is currently selected in the left-hand table. After this process is completed, GarageSale will tell you how many categories it downloaded from your eBay store.

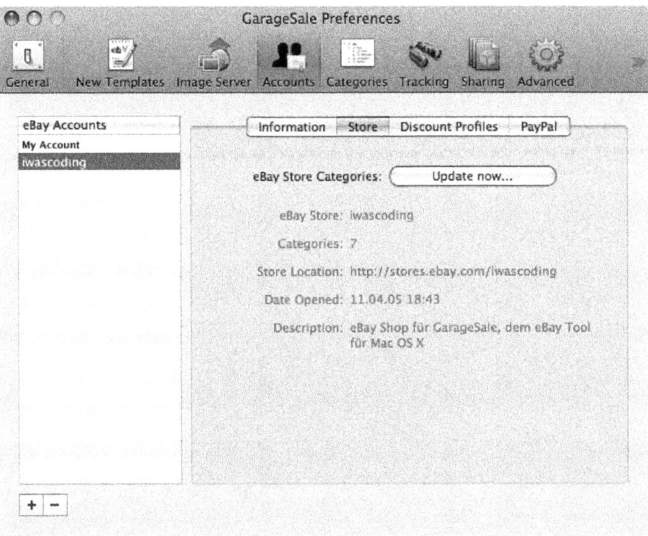

In the *Advanced Auction Options* section of the *Main Window* you can select whether to associate your auction with a category in your eBay store (enable the *Use eBay Store checkbox*) or upload an item directly to your store (enable the *List as a Store Item*, too) and not in one of the categories offered by eBay.

In the latter case, you will be able to select from a different set of durations defined by eBay for your store items.

Managing Your Running Auctions

CHAPTER 11
Tracking Auctions

After your auction has been started at eBay you can view your listing in GarageSale's Auction mode (versions older than *GarageSale 4*).

GarageSale 4, however, makes it even easier. Here again, in the same way as while setting up your auction, the convenient inspector helps you out.

(Make sure *Tracking* is activated in the *GarageSale Preferences.*)

Inspector—Tracking Auctions

In order to see any content, you have to select a template or, to track auctions, one auction. Otherwise, the inspector remains empty:

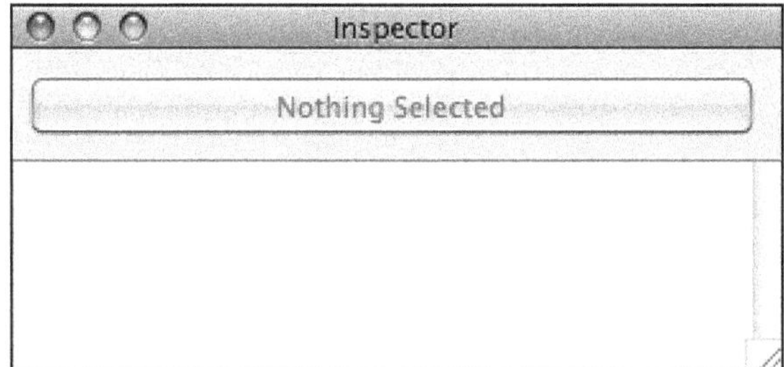

Once you have selected an auction, the inspector will always load all information automatically.

You will get all information about the auction, as well as about transactions resulting from the auction:

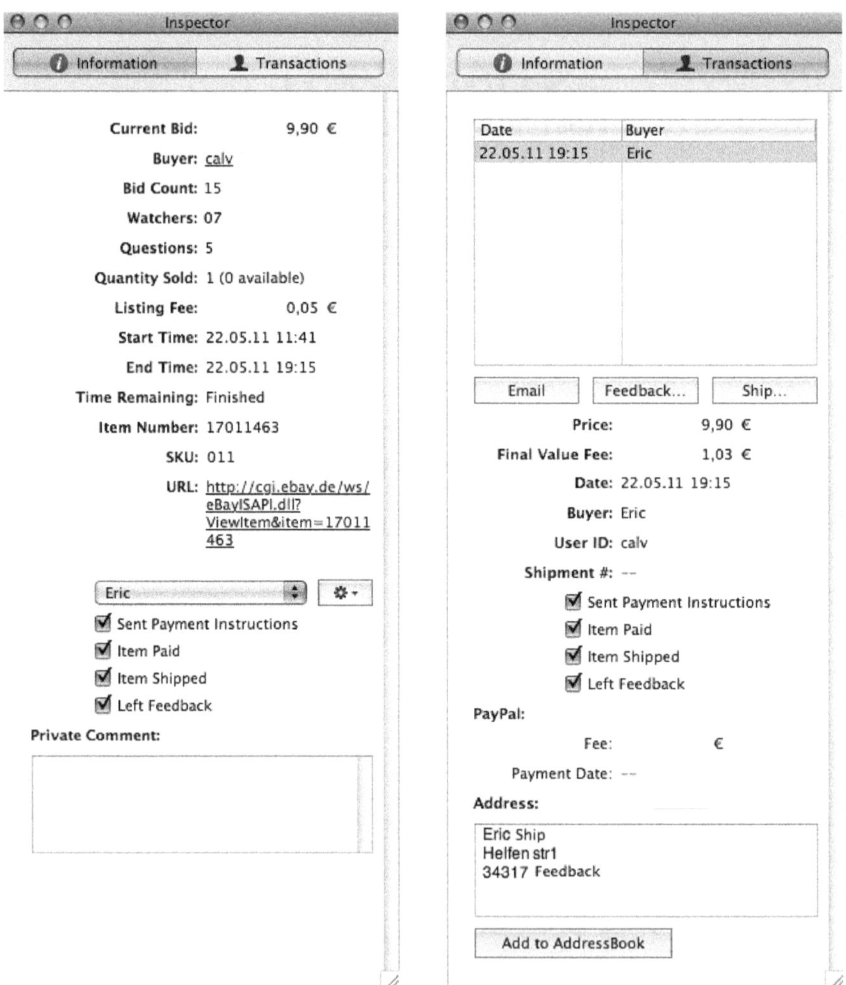

Auction Information

Once you select an auction GarageSale will display the start and the end time of your auction, the time remaining as well as the listing fee at the right side of the main window:

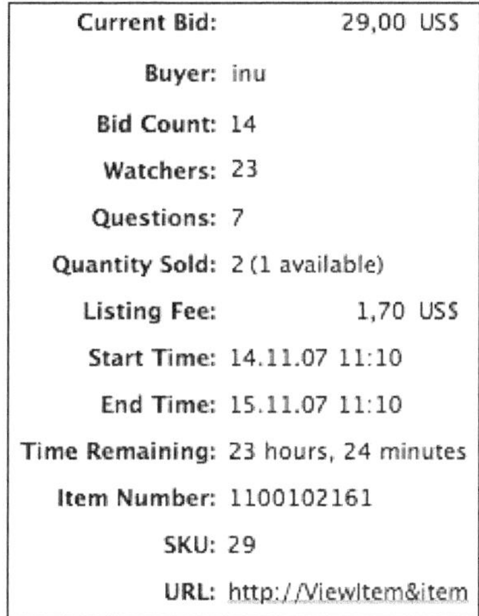

Current Bid: 29,00 US$
Buyer: inu
Bid Count: 14
Watchers: 23
Questions: 7
Quantity Sold: 2 (1 available)
Listing Fee: 1,70 US$
Start Time: 14.11.07 11:10
End Time: 15.11.07 11:10
Time Remaining: 23 hours, 24 minutes
Item Number: 1100102161
SKU: 29
URL: http://ViewItem&item

You can use the four checkboxes to track the after-auction state of your item.

The *private comment* field can be used to save remarks about a particular auction:

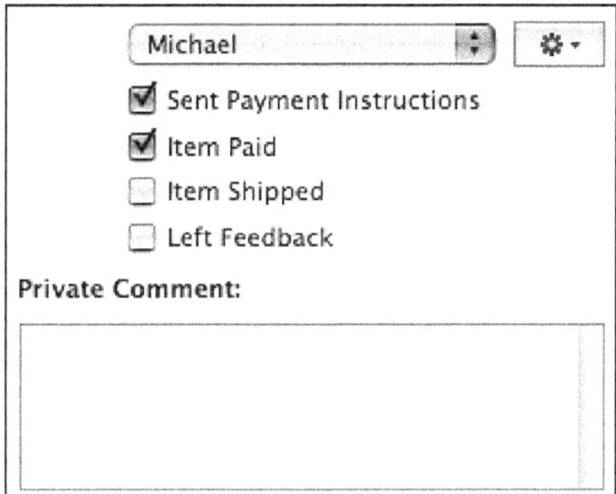

If you have enabled *auction tracking* in the *GarageSale preferences*, the application will periodically contact eBay to get information about the current highest bid and the total number of bids. Once your auction has ended GarageSale will also download the name of the buyer (or the name of the most recent buyer for multiple item auctions).

Auction Transactions

For each item successfully sold on eBay a transaction record is created. You can view the transactions for an auction by clicking on the *Transactions* segment at the lower right of the auction details pane. Here you can see the buyer's eBay ID, name, and address for each transaction for an item. You can also leave feedback by clicking on the button labeled *Feedback* below the list of transactions.

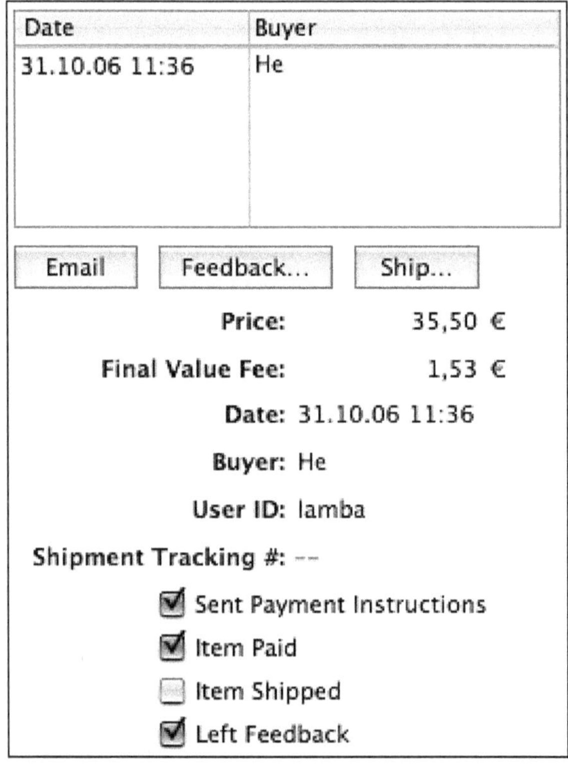

Overview Mode

When you select more than one auction in the table on the left side of the main window, GarageSale will switch to the *overview mode*. You can also use this Overview to see the current state of your auctions. Depending on whether you are in *list* or *image overview* mode, either a table with auction details or images representing your auctions will appear.

In *GarageSale 4* and newer you'll get this overview by simply clicking on *My Auctions* or on the *Overview* button in the bottom toolbar:

Those images carry small labels indicating your *auction's state*. The first number in the label denotes the number of bids your auctions has received. The second number is the current bid for your auction. A *grey label* indicates that your auction has ended successfully, a *yellow label* that your auction has begun but that no one has yet placed a bid. A *green label* means that your auction is running and has received one or more bids. A *red label* indicates an auction that has ended but didn't receive any bids.

Apart from that, your auctions can be seen in the menu on the left where the colored dots indicate the state:

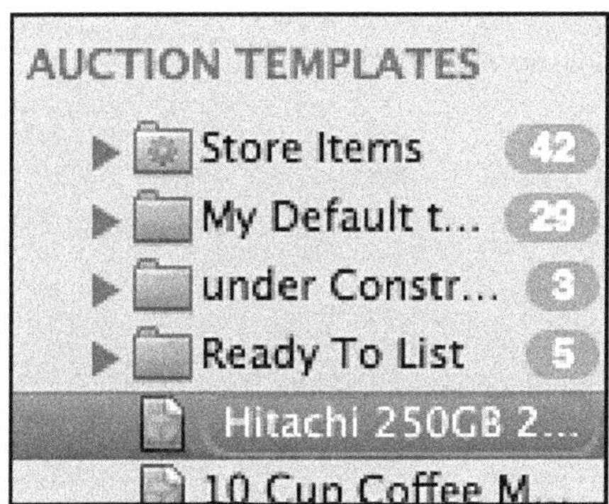

REMEMBER! The auctions can change *every minute*. Make sure you download the latest states:

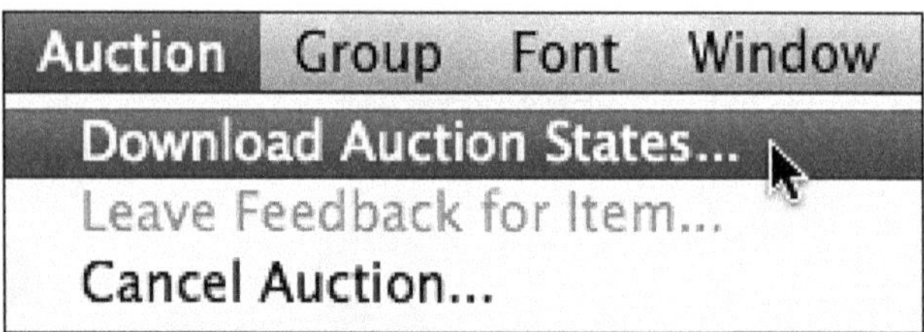

To *refresh auction states* automatically check the box in GarageSale preferences and choose the time interval:

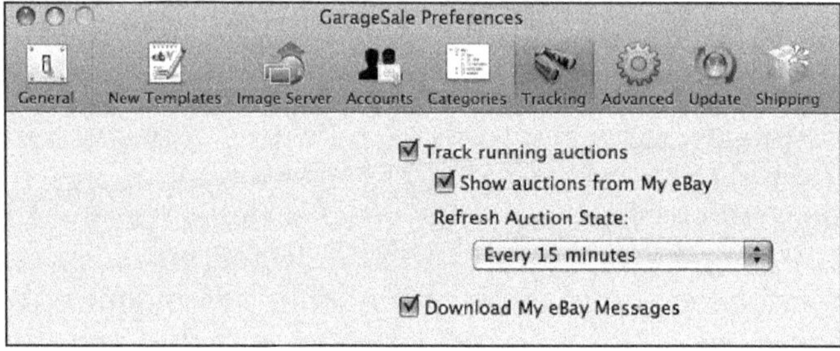

CHAPTER 12
REVISING AUCTIONS

If you need to modify a listing after you started it, you can revise your listing inside GarageSale.

To do so, switch to GarageSale's template mode or in *GarageSale 4* and newer use the *Inspector* and...

1. Select the auction template you started your listing from.

2. Make the changes you want to incorporate into your listing to the selected template.

> In *GarageSale 3*, when you are done, go to the templates *Auction* section by clicking the switch control at the top right, (NOT the mode buttons in the top middle!).
>
> In *GarageSale 4* and newer, you simply have to use the *Inspector* (look for the *Auctions tab*).

3. From the auctions table, select the auction to revise and click the *revise* button.

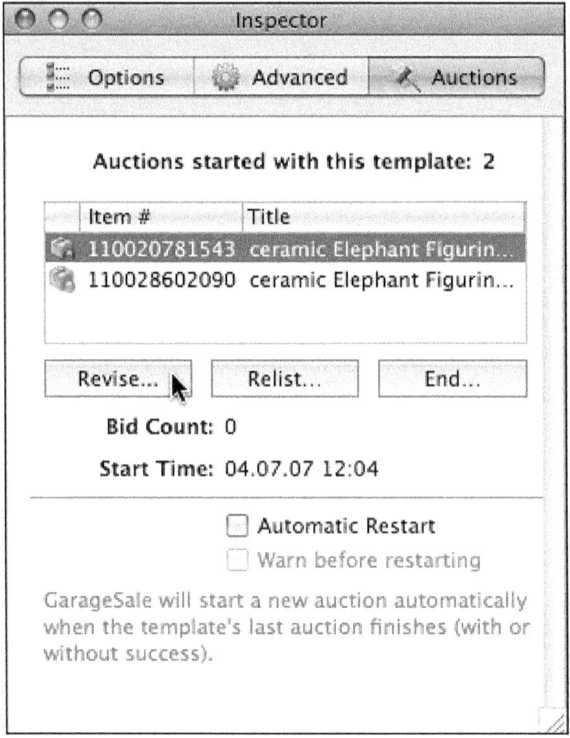

4. Now choose what parts of the auction to revise or select 'Revise entire auction'.

In case you brought up the revise panel from the menu item in the Template menu while having several auction templates selected, you can now choose what auctions in you want to revise exactly in the upper part of the window. Note that you can either select an auction template, which will include all auction started from that template in your revise, or cherry-pick individual auctions.

Revising Auctions

If you make a mistake in several of your auction listings, all is not lost. You can easily revise multiple auctions as a batch.

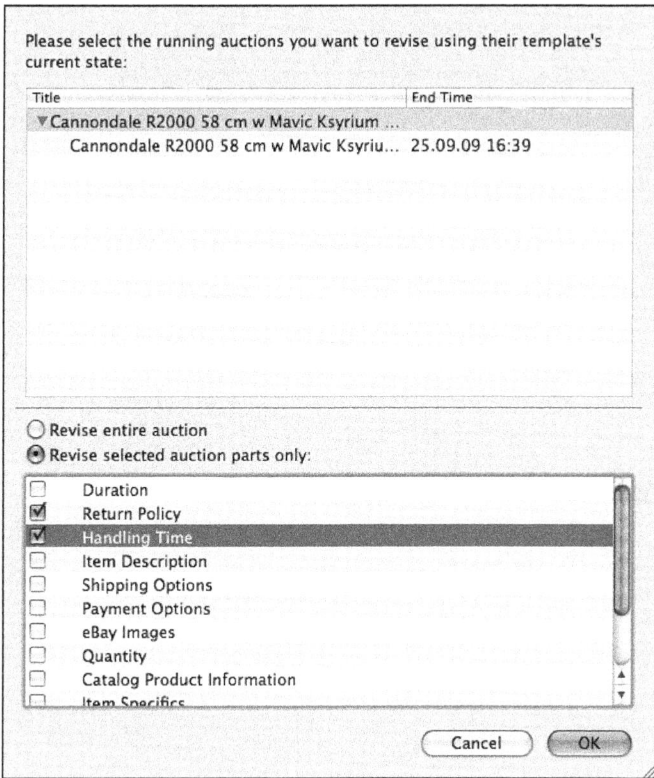

5. GarageSale will then revise your auction.

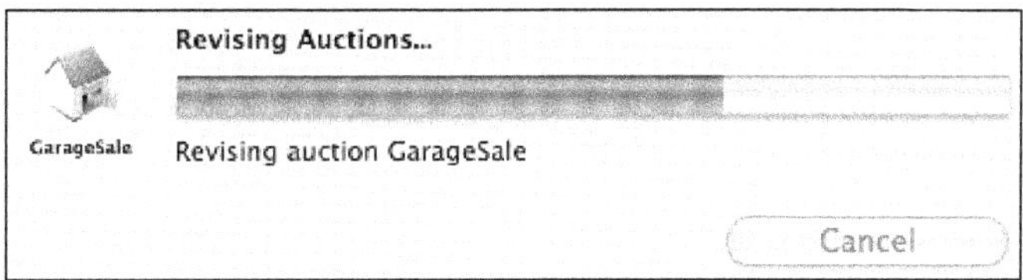

Note, there might be several reasons why eBay might not accept your modifications!!! In this case, of course, GarageSale will warn you as follows:

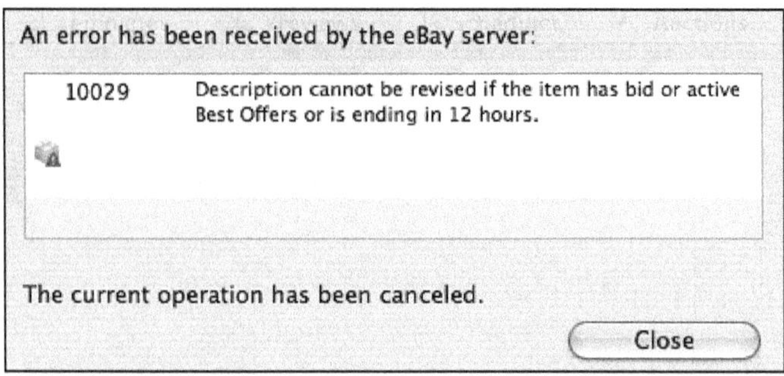
An error has been received by the eBay server:

10029 Description cannot be revised if the item has bid or active Best Offers or is ending in 12 hours.

The current operation has been canceled.

Close

You might also find the tutorial video *Revising Auctions* helpful.

Revising Multiple Auctions

In GarageSale you can also revise multiple auctions in batch. To do so select the auction templates you want to revise and from the *Template Menu* choose *Revise Running Auctions*.

CHAPTER 13
RESTARTING AUCTIONS AUTOMATICALLY

GarageSale gives you the opportunity of restarting an auction automatically after the template's last auction has finished.

To do so simply check the appropriate box:

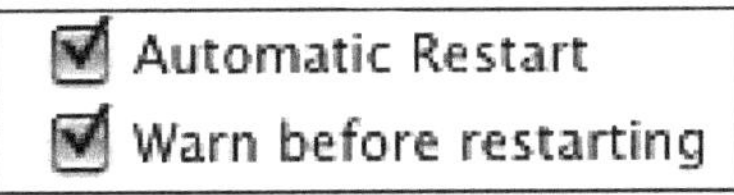

IMPORTANT: If you choose this option the auction will be restarted **regardless of the result** of the last one!

GarageSale will remind you every time you choose this option. You will get a message that looks like this:

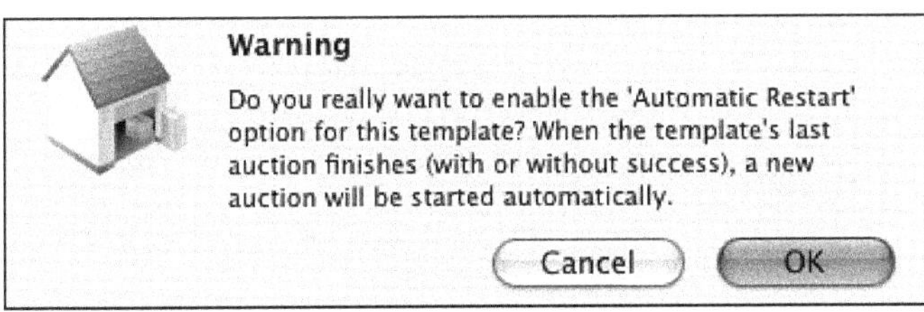

If you prefer a final warning before restarting, simply check the box as indicated above.

Of course, you can also simply re-list your auction afterwards.

CHAPTER 14
CREATING REPORTS

GarageSale enables you keep track of your budget by creating reports. These Reports can display vital information such as *Final Price*, *PayPal Fees*, *Listing Fees* and much more.

To create a report select a currently running auction and click the *Add Report* button in the toolbar.

To further *customize your report*, open the inspector. Here you can modify your report by changing its name, telling GarageSale which fields to display, setting the timeframe and even spicing up your report by choosing your own colors.

> **Making eBay Work**
>
> The key to success on eBay is to closely monitor how your auctions are doing—to learn what works and what doesn't. The key to doing *that*, is GarageSale's terrific reporting function.

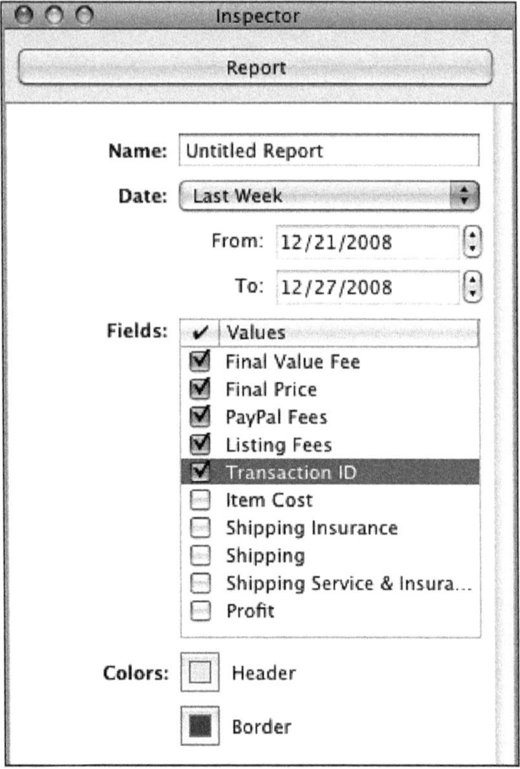

Exporting Reports

You can export your Reports to various formats: *RTF, HTML, CSV* or *TSV*. Select *Export Reports* from the *File* menu and select the desired File Format.

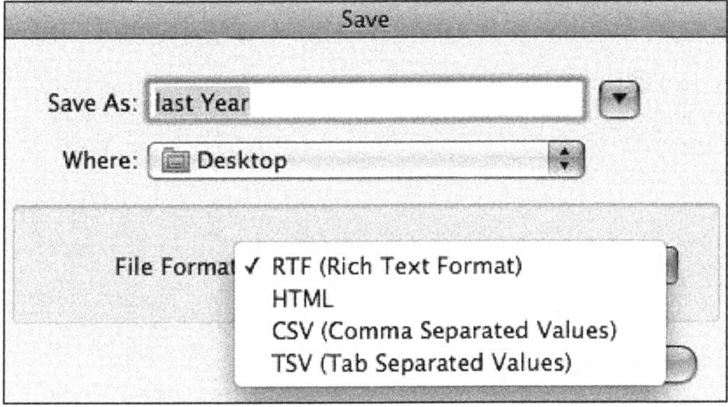
Save
Save As: last Year
Where: Desktop
File Format
✓ RTF (Rich Text Format)
HTML
CSV (Comma Separated Values)
TSV (Tab Separated Values)

CHAPTER 15
SMART GROUPS

A smart group is an "intelligent" group that contains aliases of items that fit the selected criteria for the smart group. Smart Groups are updated automatically.

Some examples:

Let's say you want to create a smart group that contains all your auction templates you want to list as store items. To do so click on the + button in the bottom toolbar:

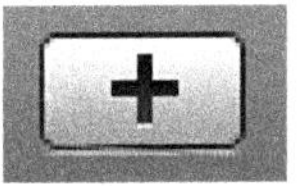

A new panels open where you can choose *Smart Group:*

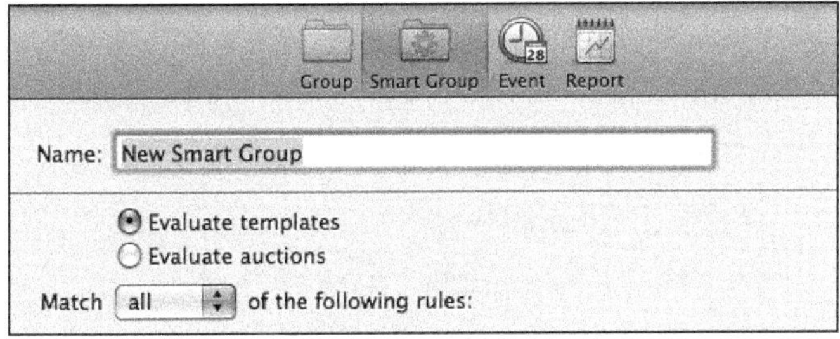

In the settings window choose *List as eBay Store Item > Is > YES.*

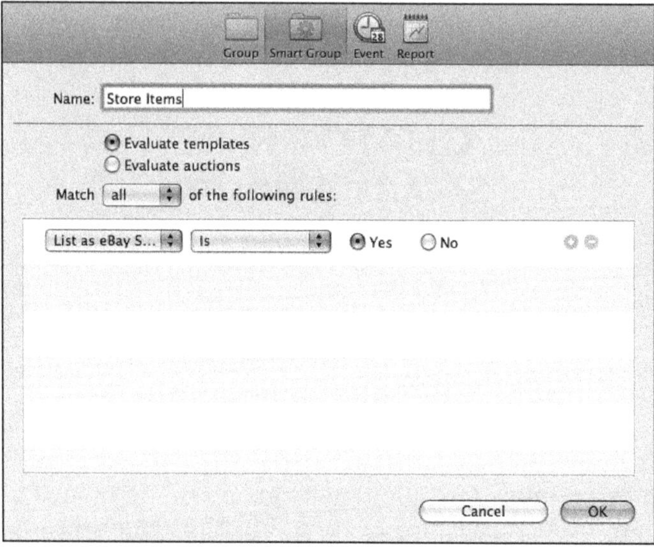

Hit the OK button and you're done. In the left list you'll now find your new smart group that contains all your store item templates in the *Auction Templates* section.

Sometimes it's helpful to get an overview of all auctions that didn't sell so you know which auctions need to be re-listed. Create a new smart group in the *Auctions* section and make the following settings:

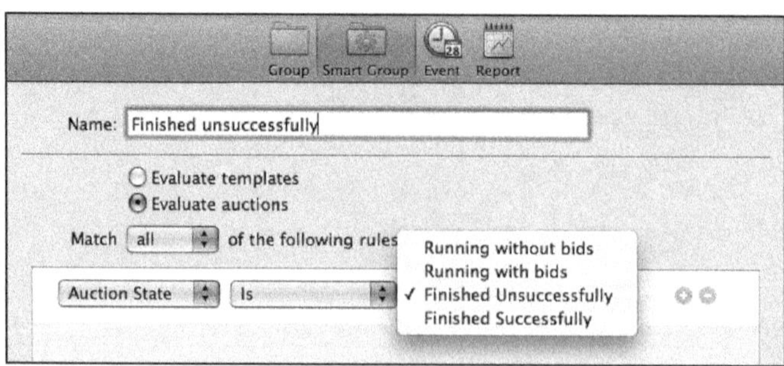

Thanks to smart groups you can easily manage and sort your auction templates and auctions.

Note that you can create smart groups under the *Auction Templates* and under the *Auctions* section.

You can change the smart group settings whenever you want. To do so just double-click the smart group icon...

to open the settings window.

Post Auction Management

CHAPTER 16
Relisting Auctions

Finished auctions that haven't received any bids can be started again without paying listing fees twice. eBay will credit you the listing fee for your original auction after your item has been sold. This procedure is called *Relisting*. To relist an from within GarageSale...

1. **Select the auction template** you originally used to start the auction (in template mode).

2. **Go to the auctions section** of the template (on the right).

Then, in the list of auctions started from the template...

3. Select the auction you want to relist and click on the *Relist* button.

A dialog will appear where you can choose if you want to relist the auction unchanged or if you want to use the changes you made to the template since you originally started the auction.

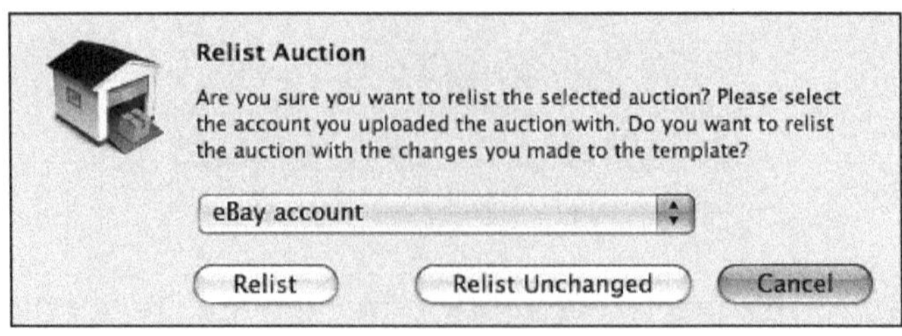

In *GarageSale 5.2 and higher* you'll also see a *Relist Anyway* button in this window under some circumstances. It lets you relist an auction even if GarageSale thinks relist criteria are not met (e.g. the item sold but the buyer didn't pay).

If you wish to relist your auction regardless of the result, consider *restarting your auction automatically* (new in version 3.1).

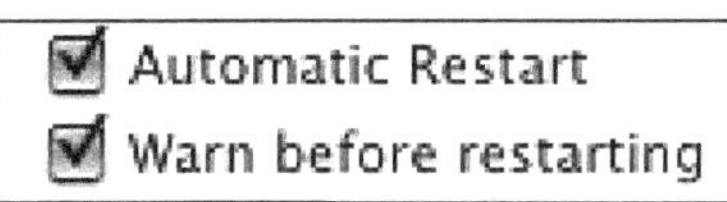

Relisting Auctions prior to GarageSale 2.3

You can relist auctions that haven't received any bids by switching to GarageSale's auctions mode and choosing Relist Auction... from the *Auction Menu.* eBay will credit you the listing fee for your original auction after your item has been sold.

CHAPTER 17
COMMUNICATING WITH BUYERS

After your item successfully sold, you want to contact your buyer to send payments instructions and keep him or her up to date on the progress of his transaction. With GarageSale you can greatly decrease the amount of time required for these tasks by using customizable e-mail templates.

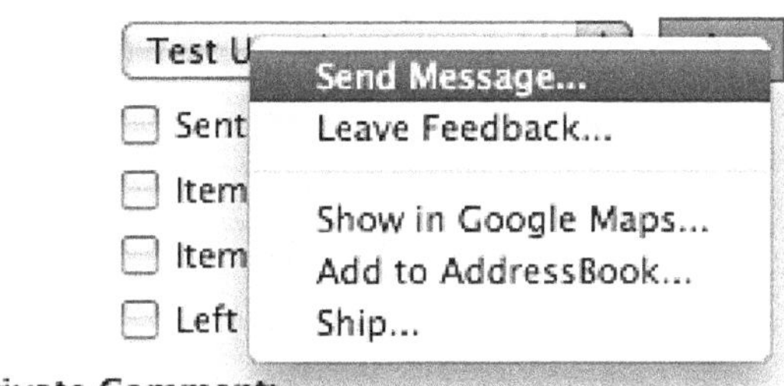

To send an e-mail to a buyer, select the auction in GarageSale's auction mode. Head over to the transaction section of the auction and select the buyer you want to send an e-mail message to from the transactions table (you can also select multiple transactions for mass mailings from this table). Click the *Email* button below the table to bring up GarageSale's *Send Mail* panel.

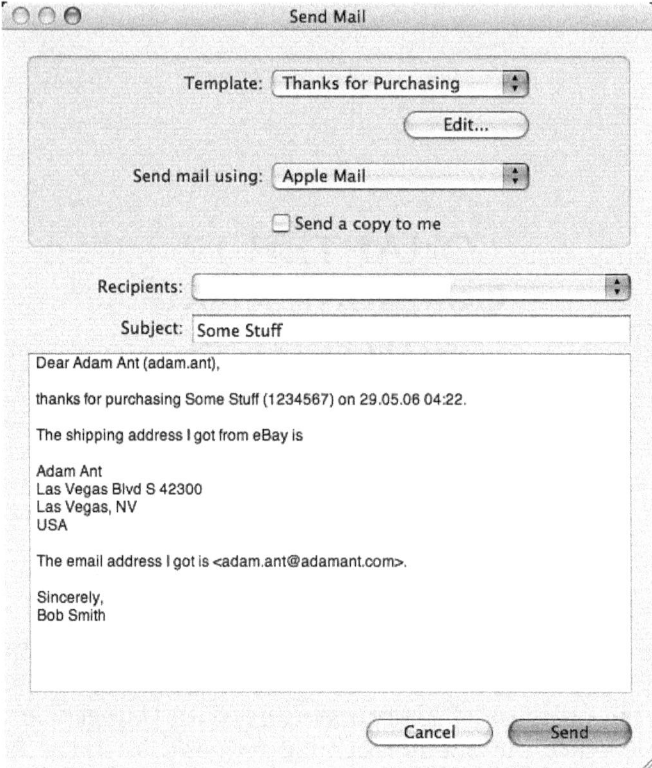

From the topmost popup menu in the *Send Mail* panel select the e-mail template you want to use. You can customize and add message templates by clicking the *Edit* button below the menu popup menu.

Specify how you want to send the message from the second popup menu. Using the *Apple Mail* message will create a new mail message in Apple's Mail application. This has the advantage of the message being added to your *Sent Message* folder in Mail for later reference. If you select the *SMTP Delivery* option the message will get sent directly to your buyer without being saved in your e-mail client.

If you activate the *Send a copy to me* option your own e-mail address will be added to the list of recipients for this message and you will receive it in your inbox.

The recipients popup menu displays all the buyers to which this message will get sent. Changing the selection in the popup menu will make the message field at the bottom of the panel display the message as it will get send to the selected buyer. If necessary you can make changes to the contents of this field.

Clicking the *Send* button will send your message to all the selected buyers.

CHAPTER 18
LEAVING FEEDBACK

GarageSale offers a powerful Feedback function that let's you leave feedback for several auctions at once.

There are two ways to invoke GarageSale's Feedback function: You can select *Leave Feedback for Item* from the *Auction Menu* to leave feedback for all transactions of the selected auction that haven't been rated by you so far.

You can also go the *Transaction* section for a certain auction, select one or more transactions, and click on the *Feedback* button to leave feedback for the selected buyers only. Both methods will bring up GarageSale's *Feedback* panel:

> **Feedback**
>
> Your feedback rating is one of the most important marketing tools you have. It is the primary way most eBay customers have of assessing your credibility as a merchant. If you do not file feedback reports for your customers, you can't expect them to do so for you.

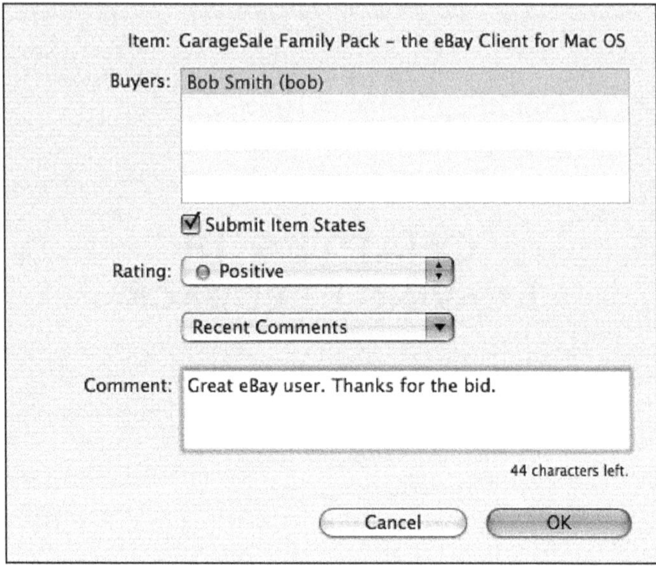

In this panel you can leave feedback for all the buyers displayed in the buyers table with just one click.

If you activate the *Submit Item States* checkbox, the current state of the *Item Paid* and *Item Shipped* checkboxes will be submitted to eBay when GarageSale leaves you feedback.

In the *Rating Menu* select the kind of feedback you want to leave. Be aware that most eBay users react less than delighted when they receive non-positive feedback.

In the comment field leave a message for your feedback rating. You can access comment strings you have recently used from the *Recent Comments* pulldown menu.

Customizing GarageSale

CHAPTER 19
GarageSale Preferences

To access GarageSale's preferences select *Preferences* under GarageSale in the *Menu Bar*.

General

Change your *eBay Site, Country, Region and Location* here . You can also change some view settings and re-enable all warning dialogs.

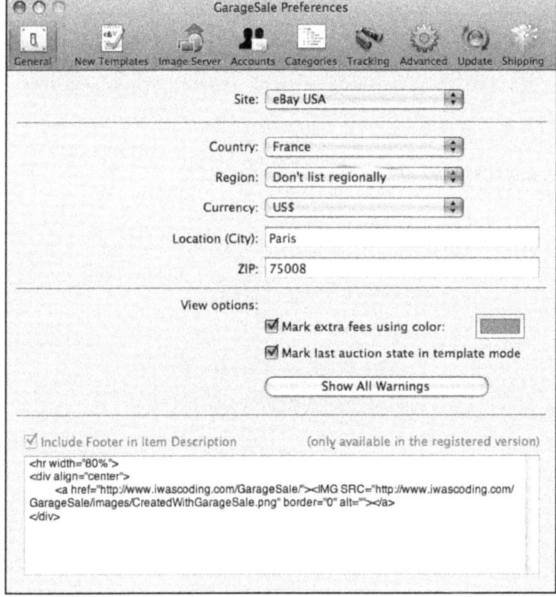

View Options

In the View Options section you can choose the color that is used to highlight extra fee options.

Use the *Show All Warnings* button to make GarageSale display warning dialogs you might have disabled in the past by activating the *Don't show again* checkbox in certain panels.

Footer

If *Include Footer in Item description* checkbox is activated, the contents of the text field below will be appended to every auction started with GarageSale. By default this field contains HTML code which appends the GarageSale logo to your auctions.

This footer can only be turned off or edited in the registered version of GarageSale.

New Templates

Choose the standard settings to be used when creating a new auction template with GarageSale. You can either specify your defaults using the various fields or activate the *Copy Settings from* checkbox and choose a template to copy all the settings from when a new template is created.

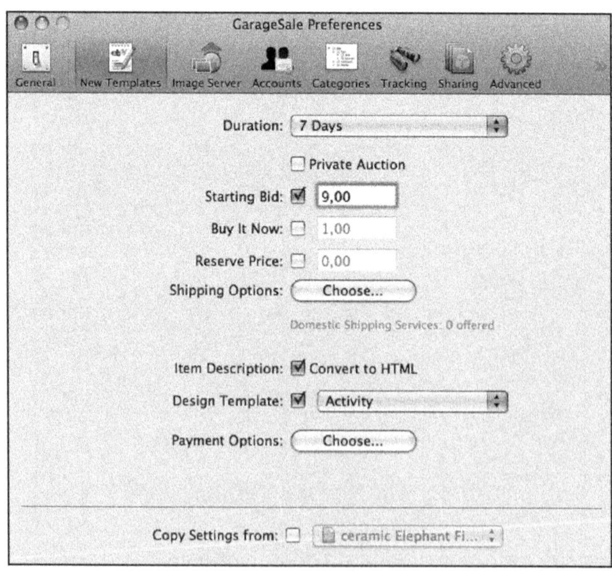

Image Server

You have 5 different possibilities of including images in your auction: EPS, .Mac, FTP, WebDAV and GarageSale's FREE Picture Service.

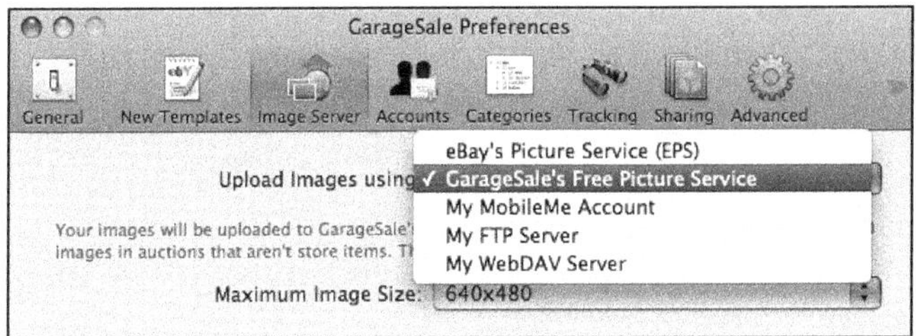

Upload images to eBay's Picture Service (EPS)

This is the default option. eBay's picture service will be used for image storage. Placing more than one image (or a larger size) in your eBay listing implies additional fees.

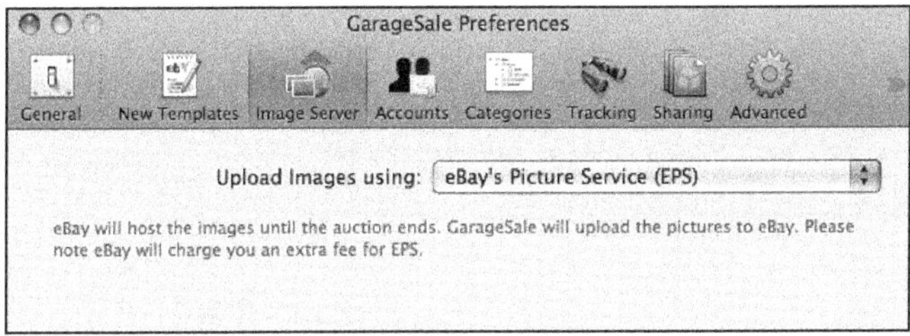

However, with GarageSale you can avoid these charges by easily using your personal web server or Garage Sale's FREE Picture Service!

Additional images can be thus used for free.

Using Garage Sale's Free Picture Service

In order to use this option select Free Picture Service in GarageSale Preferences.

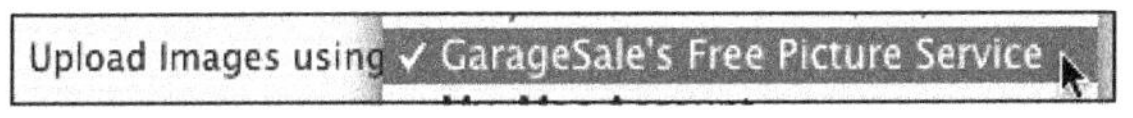

Remember that the number of pictures is **limited to 10**. If you choose more, the auction cannot be uploaded:

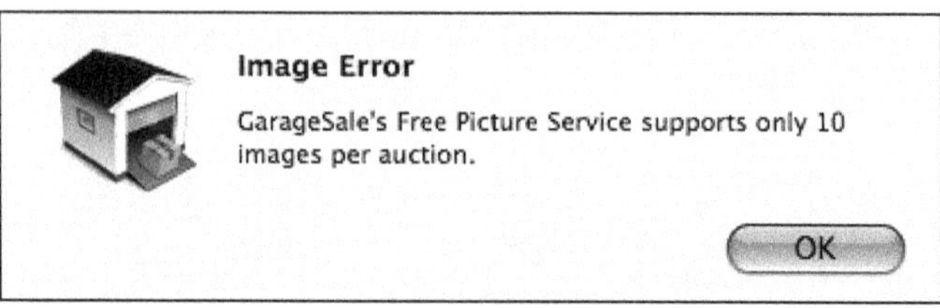

You do not need any further configuration! When you start the auction the images will be uploaded to GarageSale's image server **for free**.

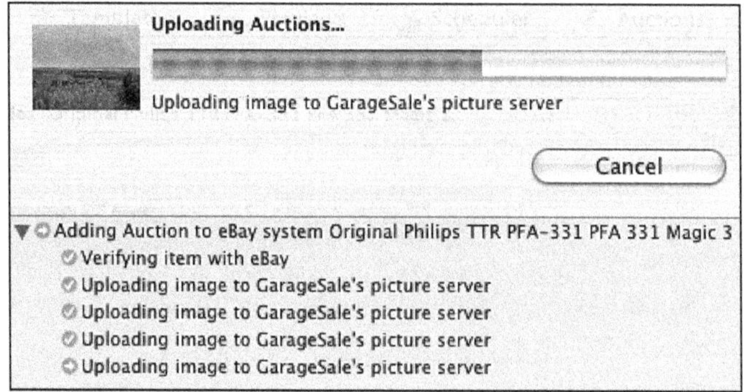

The images will remain on the server for **60 days**.

Upload images to your own web server via FTP

If you select this option, auction images will be stored on your own web server using FTP (file transfer protocol). All pictures will be included for free, regardless of the quantity or the size.

Not all servers can handle multiple connections. Disable this option if it doesn't work with your server.

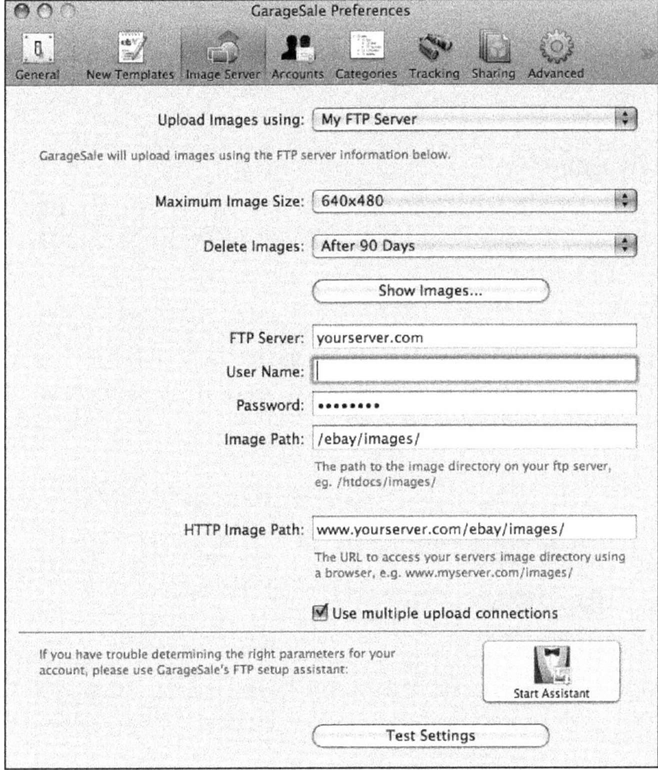

This method, however, requires a complete setup configuration:

Assistant

To make life easier for you, GarageSale can help you during the setup procedure.

The assistant will guide you through necessary steps verifying at the same time whether the data you provided is correct.

Maximum Image Size

The size you want your auction image to be scaled to before uploading.

Delete Images

You can decide whether and—if yes—when the images you uploaded should be removed from the server by GarageSale.

Show Images

Behind this button you will get a detailed overview of your uploaded images: location, the last upload time, the last time you used them and when they expire:

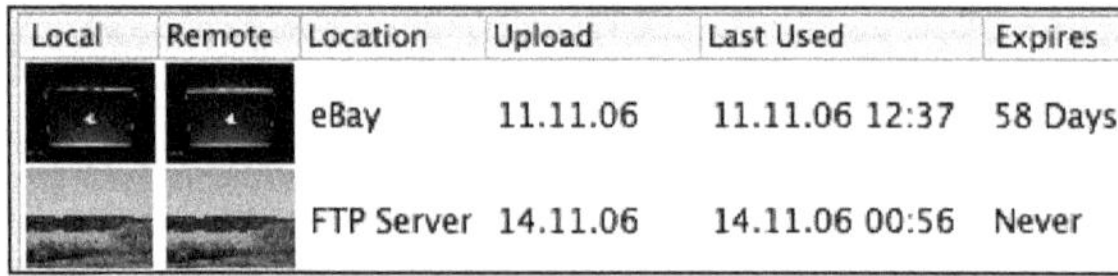

Local	Remote	Location	Upload	Last Used	Expires
		eBay	11.11.06	11.11.06 12:37	58 Days
		FTP Server	14.11.06	14.11.06 00:56	Never

Finally, you can manage the images in an easier way:

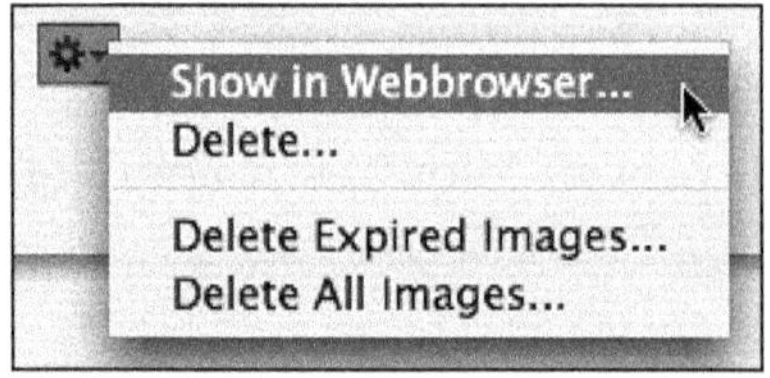

FTP Server

The host name of the web server where you have FTP access.

User Name and Password

You user name and password on the FTP server.

Image Path

The path the the directory on the FTP server where the pictures are to be stored.

This folder *must already exist*. You can use GarageSale's FTP setup assistant or one of the various FTP clients available for the mac to create this directory. On your web server, your HTML documents might be located /var/www/html. If you create a new folder *auction_images* at this location, the value for this field would be */var/www/html/auction_images*.

HTTP Image Path

The complete URL for accessing your FTP picture directory you specified as Image Path via a browser like Safari or Internet Explorer. If your image path would be */var/www/html/auction_images* and your web server would be using */var/www/html* as document directory, you should enter *http://www.myserver.com/auction_images* in this field.

Test Settings

If not already verified by the *Assistant*, be sure to test your settings before uploading an auction with separate images. This will automatically open a browser window and attempt to load a picture from your server. If no picture appears, or your browser generates an error, re-check your settings before uploading an auction.

If you are having trouble getting the FTP settings to work, please refer to the section *Troubleshooting FTP Settings*.

Upload images to own web server via WebDAV

If you select this option, auction images will be stored on your own web server using WebDav (Web-based Distributed Authoring and Versioning). When choosing your own server, be sure to complete the following fields:

Maximum Image Size

The size you want your auction image to be scaled to before uploading.

WebDAV Base URL

The HTTP URL to your images directory on your web server. This folder *must already exist*!

Login and Password

Your user name and password on your web server.

Upload images to .Mac

When this option is selected your auction image will be automatically uploaded to your .Mac account. If you already have .Mac account enter your account details in the .Mac section of the System Preferences application. If you don't have a .Mac account yet, select .Mac from the *Image Server popup menu* and click *Sign up*.

When using the FTP, WebDav, or .Mac option, only the first picture will appear above your auction description. All additional pictures will appear below the description.

Accounts

Use the Accounts section to manage your different eBay accounts. You can and add delete accounts here. Before uploading an auction to eBay GarageSale presents you with a list of eBay accounts. Choose the account you want to appear as seller next to your auction description in this popup.

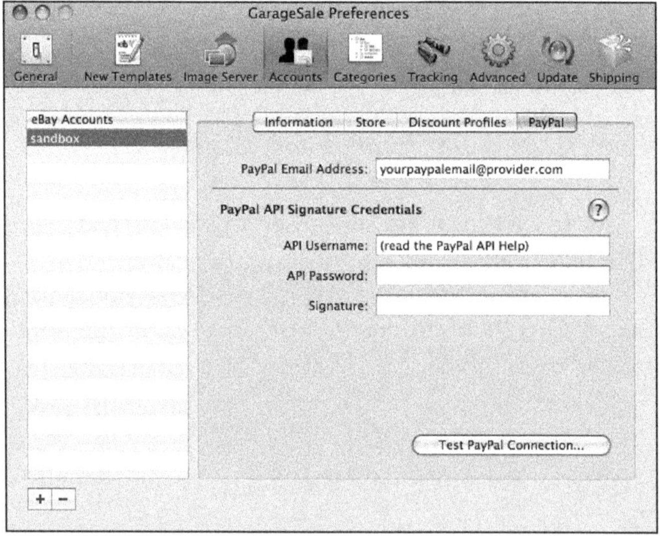

You can also refresh your eBay access token for certain accounts here. eBay tokens expire automatically after two years.

Each account may have a corresponding PayPal email address. Select the account and change the PayPal address by editing the address in the text field below.

If you are running an eBay store select your eBay account, choose the Store Tab and press the *Update now* button to download the store categories. You can later select these store categories as *Store Category*.

PayPal Integration

GarageSale 4 can monitor multiple PayPal accounts for incoming payments. See your accounts history with a single click instead of waiting for PayPal's web page to load. To use the PayPal integration you will have to follow a few steps...

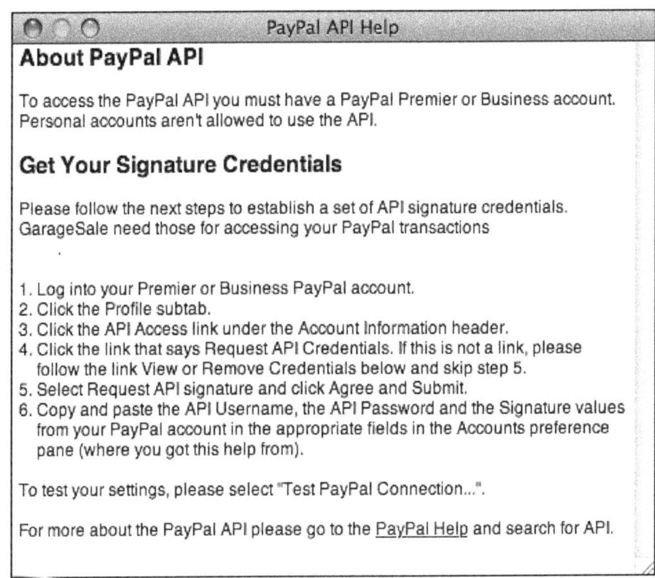

Categories

Set the frequency in which GarageSale should look for category updates on the eBay site. This is important because eBay categories do change, and an incorrect category will result in your item not being properly listed or rejected by eBay.

If you get an error regarding categories or item specifics, you've to update the category data by clicking on the *Update now* button. (Make sure the right eBay Site is selected in the GarageSale preferences>General.)

Tracking

Set the frequency in which GarageSale should refresh the auction states. GarageSale can also show and track auctions which weren't listed from within GarageSale. Just activate the *Show Auctions from My eBay* checkbox.

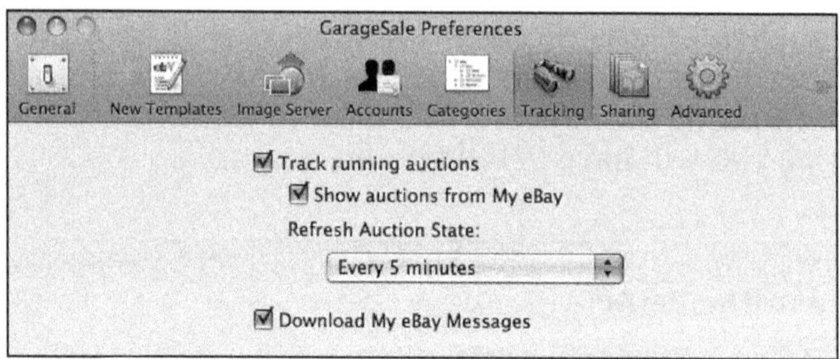

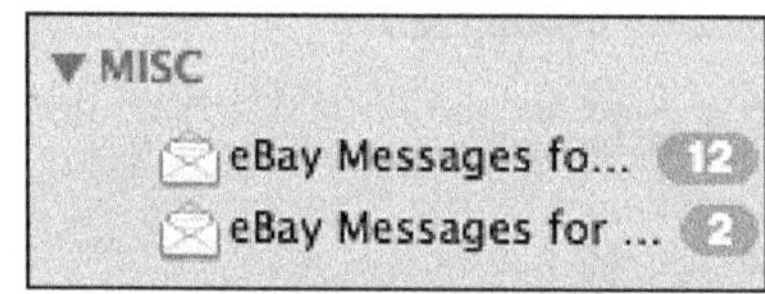

Activate *Download My eBay Messages* to see your eBay messages under the *Misc* section in GarageSale's main window in the list on the left.

Sharing

Share your prepared auction templates with other GarageSale users on your local network with Apple's Bonjour technology.

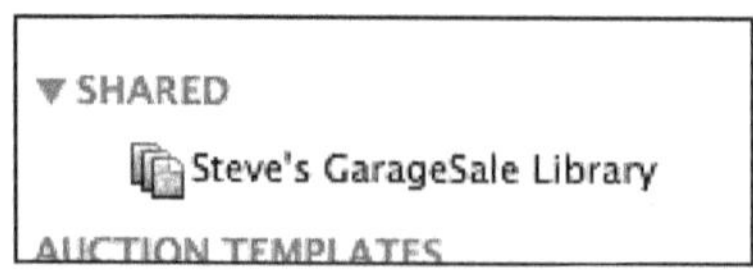

A new *Shared* section will appear in GarageSale's main window in the list on the left if another GarageSale library was found in your local network.

You can limit the sharing feature to selected groups and secure it with a password.

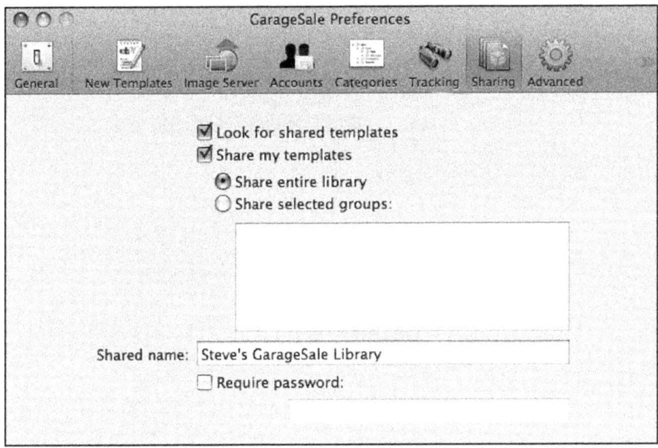

Advanced

Here you can make some advanced settings.

Delete Finished Auctions After: GarageSale deletes finished auction from its library unless you set it to *Never*.

Reduce Image Size On Import: helps you to keep your GarageSale library small.

Prevent System From Sleep: should be activated if you're using GarageSale built-in scheduler.

Remove Category After Duplication: removes the category settings from a duplicated auction templates. This way you'll never forget to set the correct category in a duplicated template.

Don't Switch Mode After Auction Start: is helpful if GarageSale should stay in template mode after you start an auction. Otherwise GarageSale will switch to the started auction.

Don't Hide Inspector In Background: Some user prefer to see the Inspector window although GarageSale is not the frontmost application.

Re-Index Library: causes the Spotlight system to re-index your auction library with the Spotlight importer plug-in shipped with your current version of GarageSale.

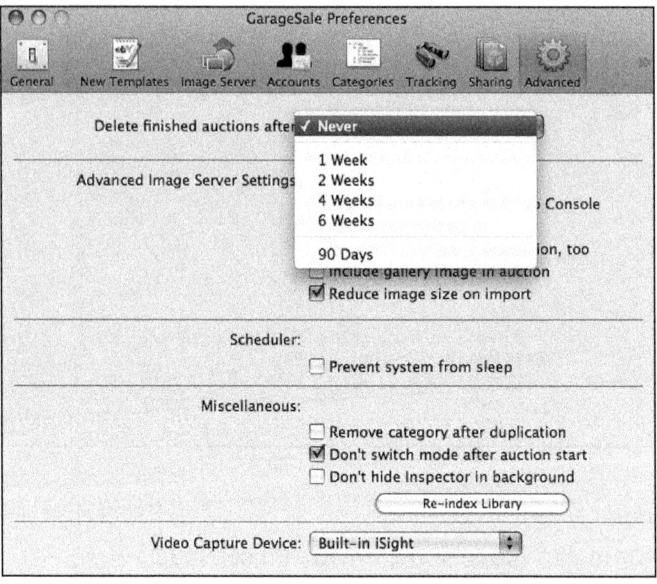
GarageSale Preferences
General
New Templates
Image Server
Accounts
Categories
Tracking
Sharing
Advanced
Delete finished auctions after
✓ Never
1 Week
2 Weeks
4 Weeks
6 Weeks
90 Days
Advanced Image Server Settings
Console
ion, too
Include gallery image in auction
Reduce image size on import
Scheduler:
Prevent system from sleep
Miscellaneous:
Remove category after duplication
Don't switch mode after auction start
Don't hide Inspector in background
Re-index Library
Video Capture Device:
Built-in iSight

CHAPTER 20
Creating Own Listing Design Templates

GarageSale allows you to create your own listing designs templates or to customize the built-in design templates.

GarageSale's design templates are folders whose names end with a *.designTemplate extension*. There have to be at least two files in a *.designTemplate folder*: Info.plist and body.html.

The body.html file contains ordinary HTML code with added commands from the *GarageSale Template Language* (See next Chapter) to include properties of the current auction template.

The Info.plist file contains information about the template itself, such as its name, its version, and a list of images used in the template stored on a remote web server.

Design Templates can be created using the *Design Template Utility* or manually.

For beginners the best way is to duplicate one of the existing design templates and make modifications to those copied files.

Locating and Storing Design Templates

You can access GarageSale's built-in templates by holding down the control key on your keyboard and clicking on the GarageSale application icon. From the popup menu choose *Show Package Contents* and navigate to */Contents/Resources/Design*

Templates. Be sure to duplicate the templates before you start modifying them.

To make Garagesale find your modified design templates, save them into the directory *Library/Application Support/GarageSale /DesignTemplates* in your home directory. If this directory doesn't exist yet, create it.

CHAPTER 21
GarageSale Template Language

GarageSale will distinguish between HTML and macro language commands using double square brackets. That means macro language commands have to be embedded in between [[and]] characters.

Commands from the macro language can be used in a Design Templates HTML text and in the *Item Description* field.

Object placeholders

Some of the macro commands are placeholders that are substituted with objects when a design template is applied to an auction description. If a placeholder refers to a string object (e.g. [[description]]) it will be replaced with that string. If it refers to another kind of object you can use a dot operator to access properties of the referred object, e.g [[item.title]].

Control Statements

The second type of macro language commands are control statements. Use these to different parts of HTML in your auction description depending on certain conditions. For example, use if for conditionals or for" loops to control the number of images in the auction.

If Statements

An if statement in GarageSale's macro language has the form [[if condition]] <code to include>[[else]] <alternate code to include> [[endif]]. The code between the the if and endif commands will only be included in your auction template if 'condition' is true, or the object it refers to is defined. Here is an example if statement that only includes an item's subtitle if the user provided one:

```
[[if item.subTitle]] <h3>[[item.subTitle]]</h3> [[endif]]
```

Foreach Statements

A foreach statement can include additional text in your template for each item in a list, for example for each image in your auction. A foreach loop has the form [[foreach item itemList loopIdentifier]]<code to include>[[endforeach loopIdentifier]], where item is used to reference an item contained in itemList each time the foreach loop is reiterated. The loopIdentifier is used to match foreach and endforeach commands when you nest several loops. Here is an example foreach statement that includes a HTML image reference for each auction image:

```
[[foreach image item.auctionImages imagesMainLoop]]
```

Since you would only want to include such a foreach loop if the user is not using eBay's picture service, it's a smart idea to check the current server setting:

```
[[if preferences.useOwnServer]] [[foreach image
item.auction Images imagesMainLoop]] <a
name="[[image.anchor]]"><img
src="[[image.imageURL]]"><br><br>[[endforeach im-
agesMainLoop]] [[endif]
```

Procedure and Call statements

If you need to same lines of HTML codes in your design multiple times, you can use the the procedure and call commands to reduce the amount of HTML code in your design.

At the beginning of your code, define your html once inside a pair of procedure and endprocedure commands like this:

[[procedure my_procedure]] my custom HTML [[endprocedure]]

Later in your code, you can use the [call my_procedure]] command to embed whatever code my_procedure conains.

Accessing Single Auction Image URLs

You can use the [[index item.auctionImageURLs i]] statement to directly access certain image URLs. Substitute i with the index of the auction image whose URL you want to include. Please note that the first image has the index 0, the second one has the index 1, and so on. This code snippnet would include the first image directly in your auction description.

```
<img src="[[index item.auctionImageURLs 0]]">
```

Testing whether an auction image index is valid

For some design templates it might be necessary to test wether the auction template contains a second image before including certain code parts in the generated HTML file. You can test wether an auction image at a certain index exists using this syntax: [[if "index item.auctionImageURLs i"]], where i is the index you are testing for. Please remember that image index counting starts a 0.

The example code below only includes HTML code for the second image if it exists:

```
[[if "index item.auctionImageURLs 1"]] <div style="bo-
rder: solid 1px #333;"><img src="[[index item.auction Im-
ageURLs 1]]" width="180" border="0"></div>[[endif]]
```

This feature only works for GarageSale 2.1 and above. If you are using the *Design Template Utility* to create your template please set the *Min. GS Version* popup accordingly.

Adding Shipping Information to your listing

If you enabled calculated shipping for your item, you can include the information you entered in GarageSale's shipping panel in your design template. Use the shipping option properties described above in the Shipping Options Properties table to insert weight and dimensions in your auction description.

```
[[ifitem.shippingOptions.usesCalculatedShipping]]<b>
Shipping Dimensions: </b><br>Weight: [[item.shipping
Options.package Pounds]] lbs [[item.shippingOptions.
packageOunces]] <br> Dimension:[[item.shippingOptions.
packageWidth]] x [[item.shippingOptions.packageLength]]
x [[item.shippingOptions.packageDepth]] <br>[[endif]]
```

For more code examples feel free to dig around in GarageSale's built-in design templates directory.

Placeholders

Design Template Placeholders

The following placeholders can use be inside a design template's body.html file.

Placeholder Name	String	Value
[[description]]	String	The description of the current auction template.
[[item]]	Auction Item	A reference to current item.
[[preferences]]	Prefer-ences	A reference to GarageSale preferences.

Auction Template Properties

The individual properties of an auction template can be accessed using these placeholders:

Property Name	Type	Value
[[item.title]]	String	The auction title.
[[item.subTitle]]	String	The auction subtitle.
[[item.minimumBid]]	String	The minimum or starting bid for the auction.
[[item.buyItNowPrice]]	String	The 'Buy It Now' price of your item.

[[item.duration]]	String	The minimum or starting bid for the auction.
[[item.checkoutInstructions]]	String	Additional checkout instructions for the item.
[[item.location]]	String	The location string for an item.
[[item.auctionImages]]	List of Images	List contains all images of the auction.
[[item.auctionImageURLs]]	List of Strings	List contains all URLs of the images included in the auction.
[[item.shippingOptions]]	Shipping Options	Shipping options.

Image Properties

The individual properties of an image can be accessed using these placeholders:

Property Name	Type	Value
[[image.anchor]]	String	A unique string that can be used to create HTML anchor and links to those anchors.
[[image.imageURL]]	String	The URL under which the item is stored.
[[image.thumbWidth]]	String	Returns either 180 or 135 depending on the image's orientation (landscape or portrait). Will always be 180 for URL based auction images.
[[image.thumbHeight]]	String	Returns either 135 or 180 depending on the images orientation (landscape or portrait). Will always be 135 for URL based auction images.

Preferences Properties

Use the preference object to query GarageSale preferences settings:

Property Name	Type	Value
[[preferences.useOwnServer]]	Boolean	True if images are stored on users own server, false if the eBay's Picture Server is used.

Shipping Options Properties

You can use the properties of the Shipping Options to include information about your shipment in your auction description.

Property Name	Type	Value
[[shippingOptions.usesCalculatedShipping]]	Boolean	True if you have enabled Calculated Shipping in GarageSale's *Shipping Options* panel for the item.
[[shippingOptions.packagePounds]]	String	Package Pounds
[[shippingOptions.packageOunces]]	String	Package Ounces
[[shippingOptions.packageDepth]]	String	Package Depth
[[shippingOptions.packageWidth]]	String	Package Width

CHAPTER 22
DESIGN TEMPLATE UTILITY

Using the Design Template Utility greatly simplifies the process of creating custom Design Templates for GarageSale. Only basic HTML knowledge is required.

The Design Template Utility can be found on the GarageSale disk image inside the Goodies folder.

You can either start from scratch or with an existing template. If you want to reuse values of an existing template, choose *Read Values from Existing Template* from the *File* menu.

To save your template, fill in the fields and click on the *Export Template* button at the lower right of the window.

The Design Template Utility

If the previous chapter (GarageSale Template-Language) caused your eyes to glaze over, then this is the chapter for you. This handy utility allows you to put together astonishingly high quality templates, and does not require you to speak in squiggly to do it.

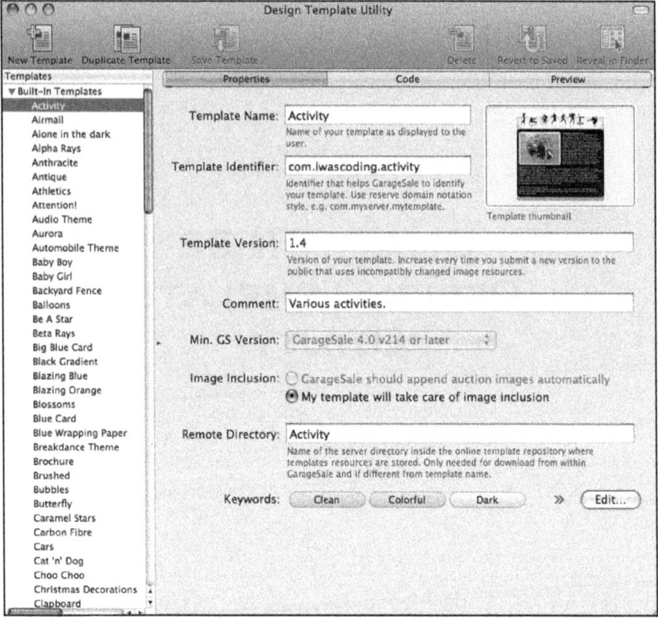

Template Name

The name of your custom design template as you want it to appear inside GarageSale.

Template Identifier

GarageSale uses this identifier to identify what design template should be used for a given auction. Please use reserve domain notation style for this field as shown in the example screenshot above. If you are creating templates only for your own use, the value of this field doesn't really matter as long as it is present and unique among all your installed templates.

If you are going to distribute your template to other users you have to make sure that your template identifier isn't already taken by another template installed on the other users machine. The best way to ensure uniqueness is to use an reserve domain notation style. Since every domain on the internet can only be assigned once, your template identifier is guaranteed to be unique this way.

For instance, if you are in control of the domain www.bills-auctions.com, your template identifiers should look like this: com.bills-auctions.template-name.

Please note that all template identifiers prefixed with com.iwas coding are reserved for the built-in GarageSale templates.

Even if you are only going to might slight modifications to a built-in GarageSale template, you should change the template identifier to make sure it your modified template doesn't get deactivated by a new version of the built-in template with a higher version number.

Template Version

Version of your template. Increase every time you submit a new version to the public that uses incompatibly changed image resources.

Comment

A comment string that is displayed in GarageSale Design Template Manager offering more information about your template.

Min. GS Version

Minimum version of GarageSale required to use this template. If you don't use any special features of the *GarageSale Template Language* leave this pop up to *Any Version*. If you are using a special feature added to the template system in a certain version of GarageSale, set the pop up menu to that version.

Image Inclusion

If your template doesn't use its own way of displaying auction images, leavc this setting to *GarageSale should append auction images automatically*. Depending on the users preferences, GarageSale will add HTML code to include images to the auction listing.

If the template has its own way of dealing with auction images, choose *My templates will take care of image inclusion.*

Remote Directory

Name of the server directory inside the online template repository where templates resources are stored. *Only needed for download from within GarageSale and if different from Template Name.*

Image Resources

A list of URLs pointing to images stored on web servers used by your template. This list is used by GarageSale to cache images and speed up preview generation. You can either add image URLs manually by clicking *Add* and filling in the table rows one by one or click on the *Extract from HTML* button after you pasted your HTML into the Template HTML field.

Template HTML

This is the HTML code you crafted in GarageSale or an HTML editor for your template. For a basic template only the [[description]] placeholder is required. This placeholder will get replaced with the users item description when an auction is previewed or uploaded to eBay.

For available placeholders and more sophisticated template designs see *GarageSale Template Language.*

CHAPTER 23
CREATING EMAIL TEMPLATES

GarageSale allows you to send messages to your buyers using message templates, which can be customized to meet your personal needs.

Go to the *Windows* menu and select *Show Mail Template* panel to bring up GarageSale's mail template editor.

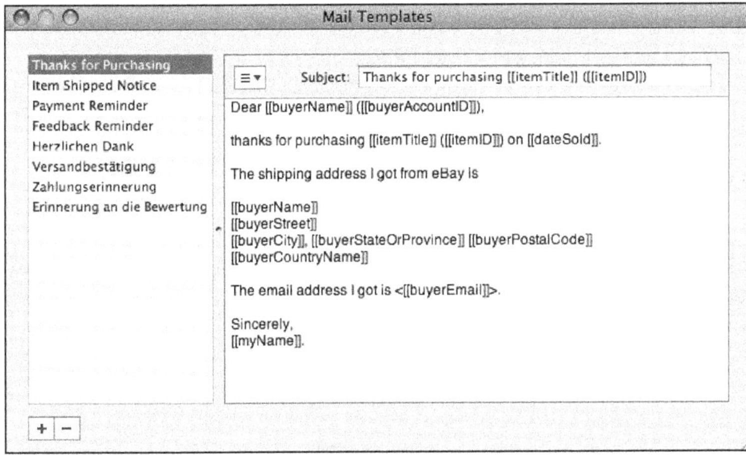

The list on the left-hand side of the window shows the available mail templates. Selecting a template will show the subject and message for the selected template on the left side of the window.

You can add or delete new mail templates by using the buttons at the lower left-hand side of the window. Rename templates by double-clicking a template's name in the list.

GarageSale allows several placeholders to be used in both your templates message text and in the message subject. These placeholders will be replaced with actual text when you send a message to your buyers. Clicking on the button on the left of the subject field will present you with a list of available placeholders. Choosing one of the placeholders from this menu will insert into the message at the current cursor position.

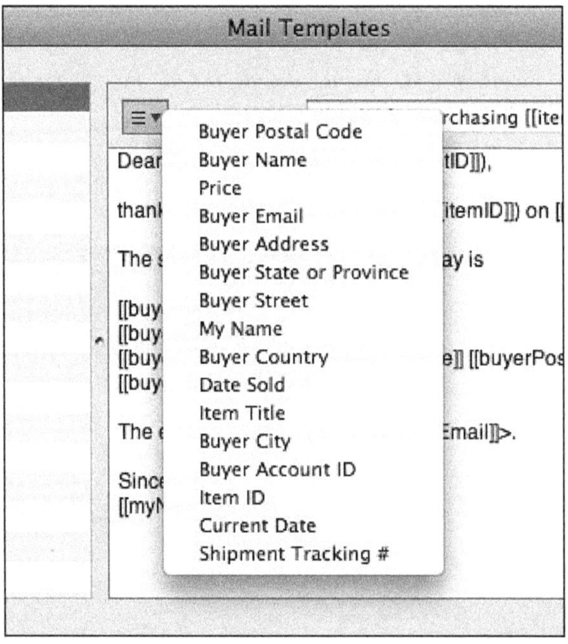

Next time you use GarageSale to send a message to a buyer the edited or newly added template will be available from the template popup menu.

CHAPTER 24
Customizing GarageSale's toolbar

Choose *Customize Toolbar* from the *View* menu to open a window with all available icons and elements:

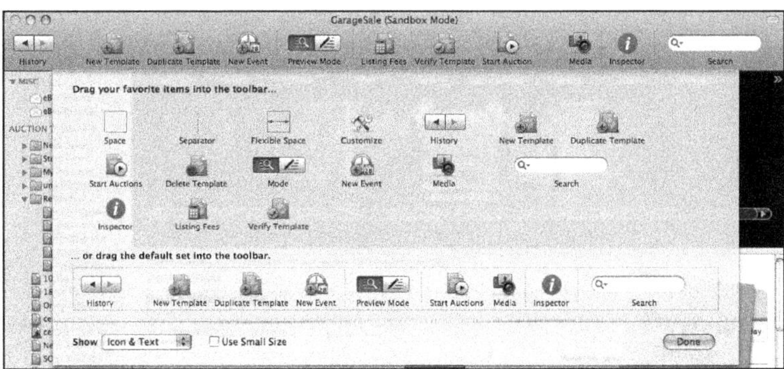

As you can do in nearly all Mac applications you can then simply drag the desired icons or elements into the toolbar, rearrange or even remove them.

You might find it useful to add the *Listing Fees* and *Verify Template* icons to the toolbar.

To get back the default toolbar just drag the default set into the toolbar.

Note: GarageSale has multiple toolbars—depending in which mode you are (*Auctions, Auction Templates*, etc.)

Customizing Miscellaneous

CHAPTER 25
APPLESCRIPT

Using AppleScript you can modify various properties of a single auction template or a group of auction template. AppleScript is a scripting language invented by Apple to automate certain task. It's more complex than using Automator actions, but has offers a greater degree of freedom.

You can use the Script Editor application to create and run AppleScripts. The Script Editor application is in the *Apple Script folder* in your Mac's Applications directory.

Applescripts

If you are not into writing AppleScripts yourself, don't forget that GarageSale comes with about 20 AppleScripts already written for you. These can be enormously time saving short cuts, so be sure to check them out.

Script Menu

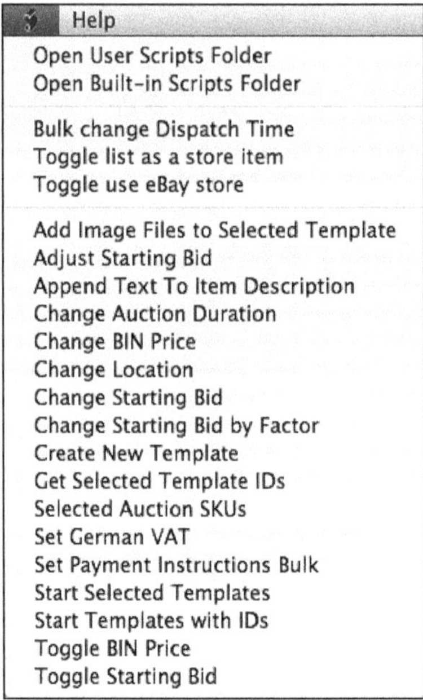

GarageSale comes with many AppleScripts pre-installed that lets you batch edit your auction templates easily.

Select *Open Built-in Scripts Folder* from the *Script* menu if you want to modify them. To install your own scripts, select *Open User Scripts Folder* and put them into this folder and restart GarageSale. More scripts created by GarageSale users can be found in the File section of the *GarageSale user group*.

Template Attributes

You can get a list of the template attributes editable trough apple script by choosing *Open Dictionary* from the *File* menu in the *Script Editor* application. Select *GargeSale Suite* and *template* to see what attributes can be edited.

Modifying the Selected Auction Templates

Use a *repeat* loop to change a certain attribute for all the selected templates (or all the templates in the selected template groups). Here is an example script that changes the starting price for all selected templates to 2.00.

tell application "GarageSale" repeat with myTemplate in the selected templates set the starting bid of myTemplate to "2.00" end repeat end tell

You can replace *starting bid* in the above example with any template attribute shown in GarageSale's AppleScript dictionary.

Modifying All Auction Templates

If you would like to change an attribute for all your templates in GarageSale, not just the selected ones, you have to *repeat* through *templates* instead of *selected templates.*

tell application "GarageSale" repeat with myTemplate in the templates set the starting bid of myTemplate to "2.00" end repeat end tell

CHAPTER 26
Troubleshooting FTP Settings

The current version of GarageSale does not support SFTP connections. Passive FTP connections and FTPS connections are supported.

If you have trouble figuring out the correct settings you can use Mac OS X's built-in FTP client.

- Open the Terminal application in the *Utilities* folder and enter *ftp.mydomain.com* and press *return* (replace *ftp.my domain.com* with your actual server name).
- Enter your user name and your password when the server requests it.
- Use the *ls* command to view the contents of the current directory and the *cd dirname* command to change to another subdirectory (replace *dirname* with the actual directory name).
- Using the *cd* command, navigate to the directory that should contain your auction images. *cd..* brings you up one directory level. When you have reached your image directory, enter *pwd* command. The printed path is the value for the *Image Path* field in GarageSale.

For further diagnosis you can also enable FTP traffic logging in the *Advanced* section of the *GarageSale Preferences* panel. Before using the *Test Settings* button from within GarageSale, open the *Console* application from your *Utilities* folder. When GarageSale performs its test you see a detailed listing of FTP commands that are being exchanged between GarageSale and your FTP server. This should help you sort out configuration problems.

Pathnames for photo files should not contain spaces. For example, the path *http://domainname.com/directory/a photo* will not preview in GarageSale. Instead, try *http://domainname.com/directory/a_photo* which should work.

CHAPTER 27
XML IMPORT FORMAT

Starting with version 3.3 GarageSale supports importing XML files in the format specified below. You can create files in this format to import listings from other sources into GarageSale. Use the *Import Templates* command from the *File* menu to import XML files.

File Layout

A single XML file can contain multiple listings descriptions. See below for the support item fields. Most fields are optional. If a listing property is not specified in the XML file, the default value you specified in GarageSale's preferences will be used instead.

Sample XML File

Here is a very simple sample XML file:

<items> <item> <title>My Listing Title</title> <description><![CDATA[My <b> great </b> stuff.]]></description> <startingBid>2.99</startingBid> <imageURL

isGalleryImage="true">http://www.iwascoding.com/GarageSale/ListingDesigns/images/Packs/Pack24/Spooky.jpg </imageURL> <imageURL>http://www.iwascoding.com/GarageSale/ListingDesigns/images/Packs/Pack24/VintageCollage.jpg</imageURL> <domesticShippingService serviceFee ="12.00" serviceAdditionalFee="2.00">UPS Ground</domesticShippingService> <internationalShippingService serviceFee="22.00">UPS Worldwide Express</internationalShippingService> <siteName>eBay USA</siteName> <design>

Be A Star</design> <layout>thumb gallery</layout> </item> </items>

Supported Item Attributes

buyItNowPrice

Provide this field if you want your listing to carry a Buy It Now price. Not providing a starting bid for the same listing will make this a fixed price auction.

category

The id of the primary eBay category you want to post your item in.

category2

The id of the secondary eBay category you want to post your item in.

convertDescriptionToHTML

A boolean value (*true* or *false*) specifying wether GarageSale should convert the item's text formatting to HTML when posting the listing to eBay.

description

The item's description.

design

The name of the GarageSale auction design you want to use.

domesticShippingService

The name of an domestic shipping service. You can add a maximum of 3 services including the services specified in Garage-Sale's *Preferences*.

Field Attributes

serviceFee—The name of an domestic shipping service. You can add a maximum of 3 services including the services specified in GarageSale's *Preferences*.

serviceAdditionalFee—The name of an domestic shipping service. You can add a maximum of 3 services including the services specified in GarageSale's *Preferences.*

duration

The duration of the auction in days (e.g. 1,3,5,7 or 10).

imageURL

(Can be specified multiple times for an item.)

An URL to an existing image file on your server. The specified URL will be added to your GarageSale template as an URL-based image and added to your auction when it is launched. Requires *GarageSale 3.4* or later.

Field Attributes

isGalleryImage—A URL to an existing image file on your server. The specified URL will be added to your GarageSale template as an URL-based image and added to your auction when it is launched. Requires *GarageSale 3.4* or later.

internationalShippingService

The name of an international shipping service. You can add a maximum of 3 services including the services specified in GarageSale's *Preferences.*

Field Attributes

serviceFee—The name of an international shipping service. You can add a maximum of 3 services including the services specified in GarageSale's *Preferences.*

serviceAdditionalFee—The name of an international shipping service. You can add a maximum of 3 services including the services specified in GarageSale's *Preferences.*

layout

The name of the layout of the design you want to use.

listAsStoreInventory

A boolean value (*true* or *false*) specifying wether you want to list your item as inventory item in your store. The *listInStore* field has to be enabled, too, in order to use this option.

listInStore

A boolean value (*true* or *false*) specifying wether you want to associate the listing with a certain category in your eBay store.

location

The location of your item.

packageDepth

The item's package depth in inches.

packageLength

The item's package length in inches.

packageOunces

The ounces of the item's shipping weight. Use the package-Pounds field to specify the pounds part of the weight.

packagePounds

The pounds part of the item's shipping weight. Use the pack-ageOunces field to specify the ounces part of the weight.

packageWidth

The item's package width in inches.

paymentInstructions

Optional payment instructions

privateAuction

A boolean value (*true* or *false*) specifying wether you want to list your item as private auction.

quantity

The item quantity you are selling. If omitted, a quantity of 1 is assumed.

reservePrice

The listing's reserve price.

siteName

The name of the eBay site you want to use for the listing. Site name has to be specified as displayed in GarageSale's *Preferences* (English Version).

SKU

A user specified item number that will be posted to eBay.

startingBid

The listing's starting price. Specify this value if you want to list your items as regular option.

storeCategory2Name

The name of a secondary store category the items should be associated with. The specified category has to be downloaded in GarageSale.

storeCategoryName

The name of the store category the items should be associated with. The specified category has to be downloaded in GarageSale.

subTitle

The listing's subtitle.

title

The listing's title. This field is required.

zipCode

The ZIP code of the item's location. Required if you want to enable location based search for your listing.

CHAPTER 28
GarageSale Icon Legend

Icons explained: Different colors and signs symbolize the state of your Auctions and Auction Templates. Have a look at this legend for details:

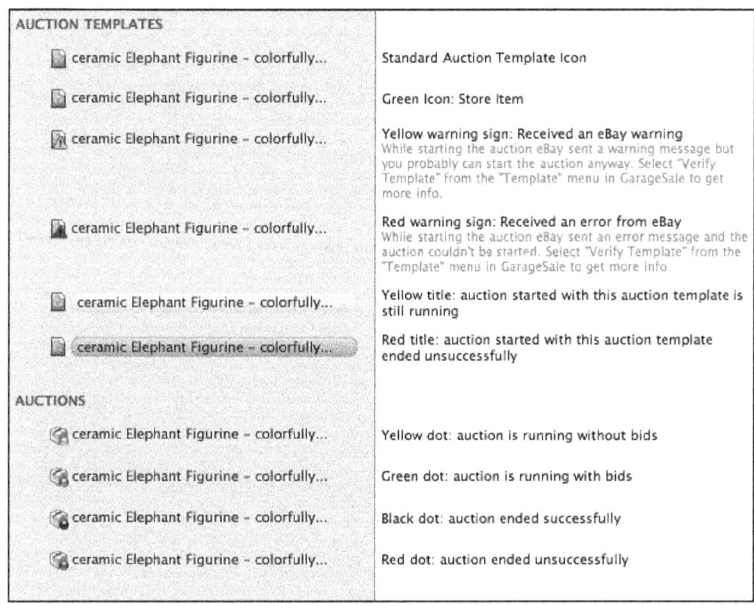

If you get a yellow warning sign when trying to start an auction eBay returned a warning about some aspect of your auction. You can choose to ignore it and still list your item. Select *verify template* from the *Template Menu* for details.

If you get a red warning sign: eBay refuses to list your item for a certain reason. Maybe verifying your templates sheds some light on this. If you don't get a helpful error message from eBay, try to list the exact same auction on the eBay webpage. Sometimes this result in a more informative message than the one eBay provides third party applications like GarageSale with.

Customizing Command Reference

CHAPTER 29
GarageSale Menu

About GarageSale

Displays GarageSale's about box showing the current version of GarageSale as well as your licensing details.

Preferences

Opens GarageSale's *Preferences* panel which lets you adapt GarageSale to your personal needs.

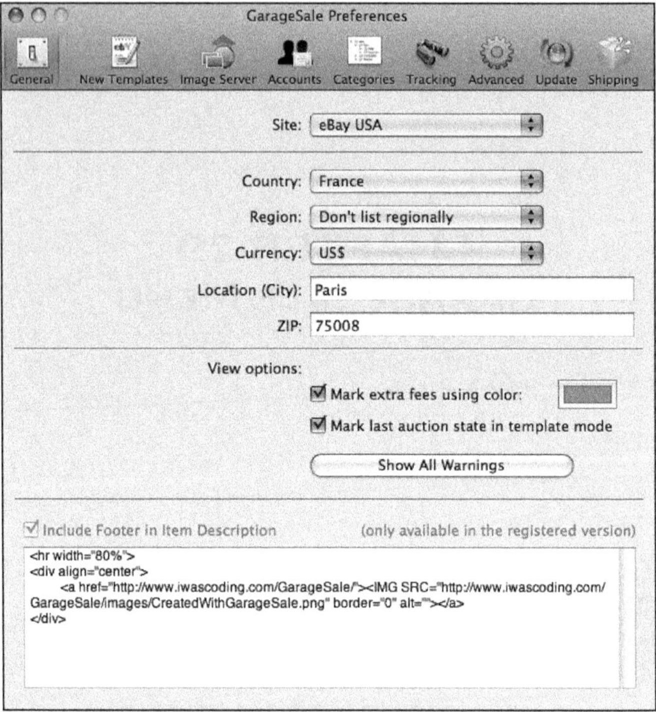

Enter License Code

Shows a window which lets you enter your existing license information for GarageSale. This window will also provide you with instructions on how to obtain a GarageSale license in case you don't own one already. This menu item is only available if you not yet entered your license information.

Install Widget

This menu item installs the GarageSale Dashboard Widget for your account as well as the GarageSale Helper application which will update the widget if GarageSale is not running.

If the Widget does not work properly, please check the following:

- Install the latest widget (Select *Install Widget* from the *GarageSale menu*)
- Make sure *Tracking* is enabled in the GarageSale preferences
- Allow *GarageSaleHelper* keychain access when prompted
- Sometimes restarting the Mac does the trick as well.

CHAPTER 30
FILE MENU

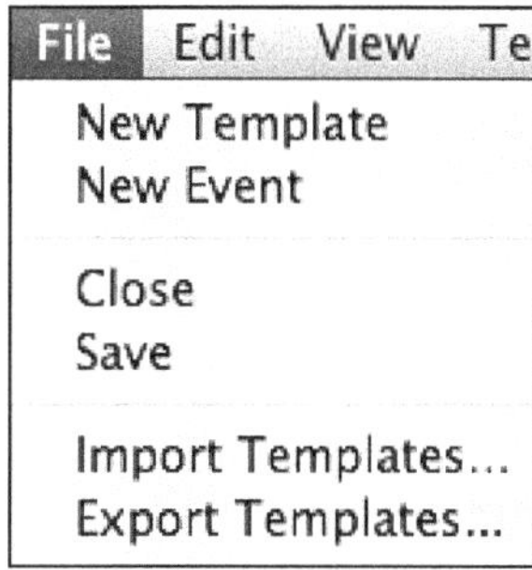

New (Command-N)

Will create a new auction template when GarageSale is in Auction or Preview Mode. Attributes for new templates can be preset in the *New Templates* section of GarageSale's *Preferences* panel.

Will create a new event when GarageSale is in Scheduler Mode. Not available in Auction Mode.

Close (Command-W)

Will close the currently active window. If this is was the only currently open window, GarageSale will quit.

Save (Command-S)

This menu item will save your unsaved changes. GarageSale will automatically save your settings when your quit the application or periodically when you have Auto Save option enabled in GarageSale's *Advanced Preferences.*

Import Templates (Command-Shift-I)

Will import previously exported GarageSale auction templates.

Export Templates (Command-Shift-E)

Will export the currently selected auction templates to either separate files or a single file. Resulting files can be used for auction template sharing or for backup purposes.

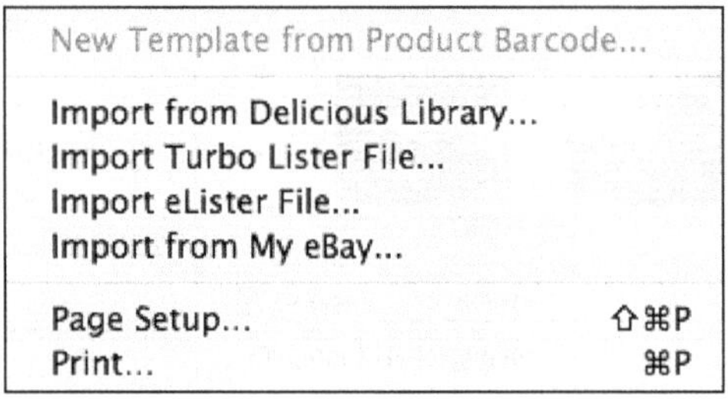

New Template from Product Barcode...

Import from Delicious Library...
Import Turbo Lister File...
Import eLister File...
Import from My eBay...

Page Setup... ⇧⌘P
Print... ⌘P

New Template from Product Barcode

Use this menu command to switch GarageSale into batch template creation mode which uses your external iSight or FireWire camera to read product barcodes and search corresponding products in eBay's product catalog. Each time a barcode is recognized a catalog search in eBay's product catalog is started. If this search returns a matching product a new auction template is created and linked to the found product.

This menu item is only available in Templates mode. An auction template which is catalog enabled has to be selected in GarageSale before this menu item can be invoked. See *Listing with Pre-filled item information* for more info about listing items with information from eBay's product catalog.

Import from Delicious Library

Users of the *Delicious Library* application can use this menu command to create auction templates from the contents of their Delicious Library database. This menu item is only available in Templates mode.

Import from Turbo Lister file

Use this menu command to import CSV (comma separated value) files written by eBay's TurboLister for Windows software. Files have to exported for *File Exchange to Turbo Lister* in Turbo Lister. The exported files should comply with this eBay defined format.

Import eLister file

Imports an eLister file.

Import from My eBay

This menu item will display a panel which lets you create GarageSale auction templates by importing your auctions running on eBay right now. (To activate all checkboxes at once just alt-click on one of the checkboxes.)

Page Setup

You know this one.

Print

Print different views of GarageSale. According to what is marked or where the cursor is placed you can print different information or images. We recommend to use the preview mode to see the result in advance.

CHAPTER 31
EDIT MENU

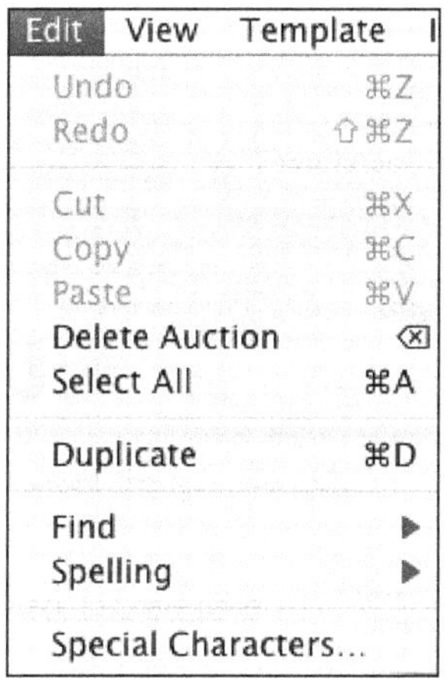

Delete Auction / Template

According to the GarageSale mode you are in, this menu item will delete either the selected template or auction.

Duplicate ⌘-D

Instead of retyping every detail of your template you can save time, simply duplicate it and make the few modification afterwards.

Spelling

You can make GarageSale check your spelling.

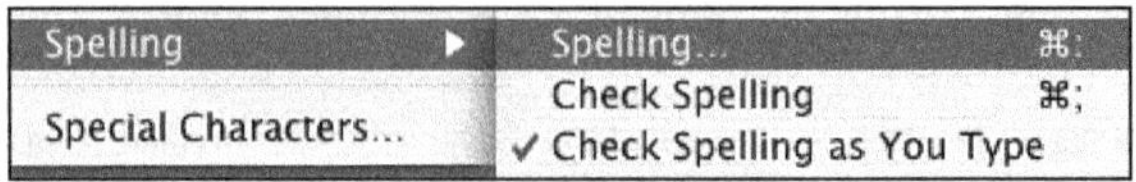

In order to select your language click on *Spelling* (⌘:).

To check Spelling select *Check spelling* (⌘;).

To make GarageSale *check spelling as you type* activate the appropriate menu command.

Special Characters

Opens a *character palette* to let you select special characters.

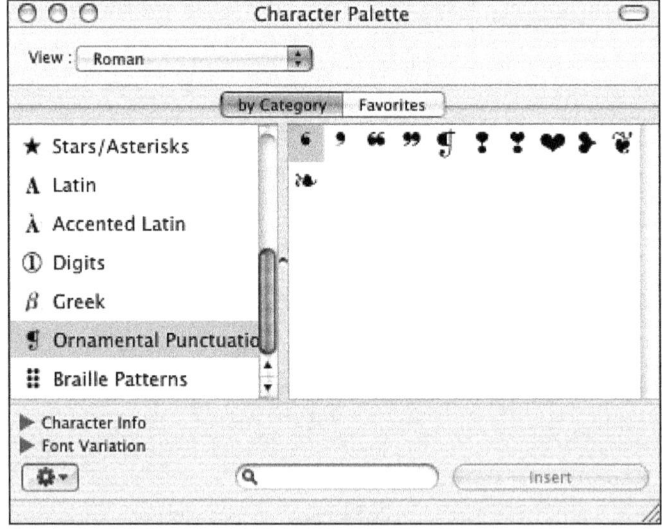

CHAPTER 32
VIEW MENU

Overview Mode

Select an item from this item's submenu to change the way GarageSale display's multiplc item selection.

Images

When selected, GarageSale will display thumbnails representing the selected auction templates or auctions. When displaying auctions, badges containing the current bid and bid count of the auction will be displayed in the thumbnails.

Table

When this menu item is selected, GarageSale will display a list of the selected items when multiple items are selected. Depending on the current application state, different columns for the item properties will be available. Use the column headers to sort your auction or auction templates according to a certain attribute.

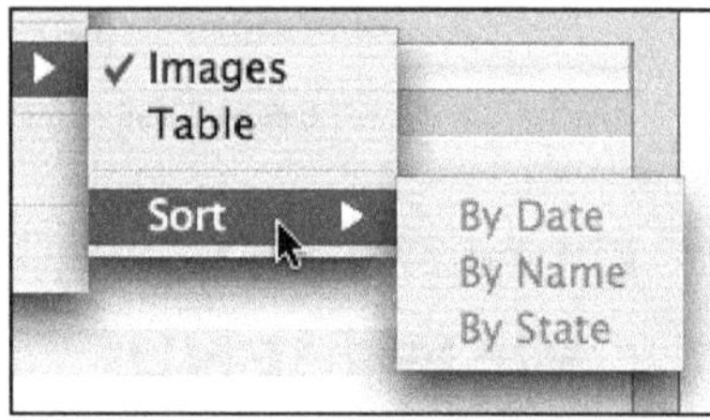

Switch to Classic Editor

Menu command and shortcut to switch to *Editor mode.*

Options Inspector

Opens the *Options* pane of the template Inspector.

Advanced Inspector

Opens the *Advanced* pane of the template Inspector.

Auctions Inspector

Opens the *Auctions* pane of the template Inspector.

Mark Extra Fees

When a check mark appears next to this menu item's title, GarageSale will highlight the names of auction options eBay will charge you extra for. The highlight color (default is red) can be changed in GarageSale's *General Preferences.*

Customize Toolbar

Lets you customize the toolbar: Rearrange, add or remove icons. (See *Customizing GarageSale's Toolbar.*)

GarageSale 3 only:
Templates

Switches GarageSale to *Templates Mode.*

Previews

Switches GarageSale to *Previews Mode.*

Scheduler

Switches GarageSale to *Scheduler Mode.*

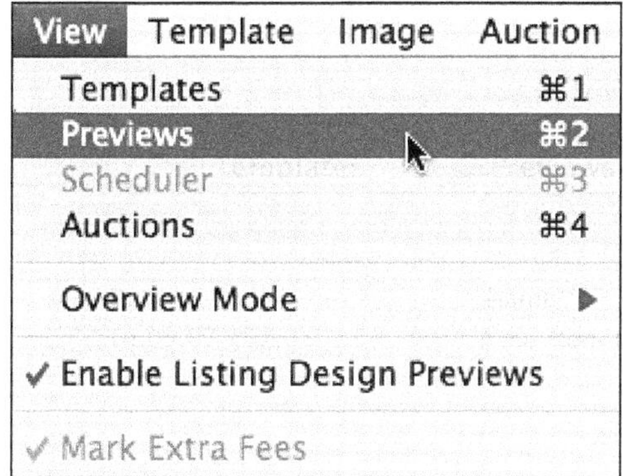

Auctions

Switches GarageSale to *Auctions Mode.*

Enable Listing Design Previews

When activated, GarageSale will display and dynamically update thumbnails of all the available design templates when a single design template is selected in *Previews Mode.*

CHAPTER 33
TEMPLATE MENU

Commands in this menu work with or affect properties of the selected auction templates. Therefore the commands are only available in Templates or Previews Mode.

Start Auction

This menu item will start auctions for the selected auction templates. When a group of templates is selected, an auction is started for every single auction template in the group. Before the auctions are started, a panel is presented where the number of auctions to be started is displayed and the eBay account that should be used can be selected.

Verify Auction Template

When this menu command is invoked GarageSale will verify each of the selected auction templates with eBay and display possible errors or warnings returned by eBay.

Edit Item Description

When invoked, GarageSale's Description Editor will be opened. It provides you with a text field to edit your item description, a automatically HTML preview of your description as well as commands to insert often-used HTML tags in your description.

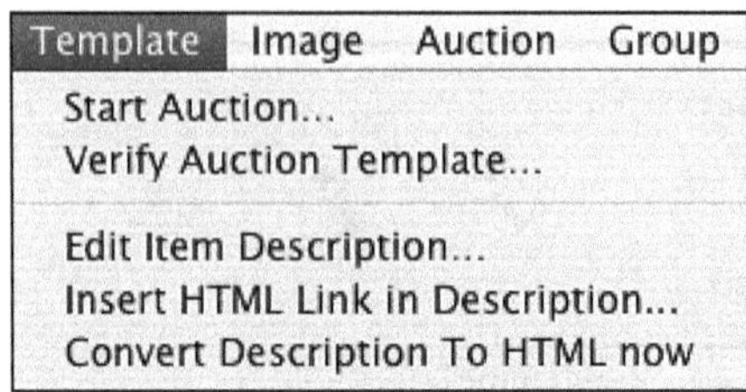

Insert HTML Link in Description

You can enter the URL and the visible text.

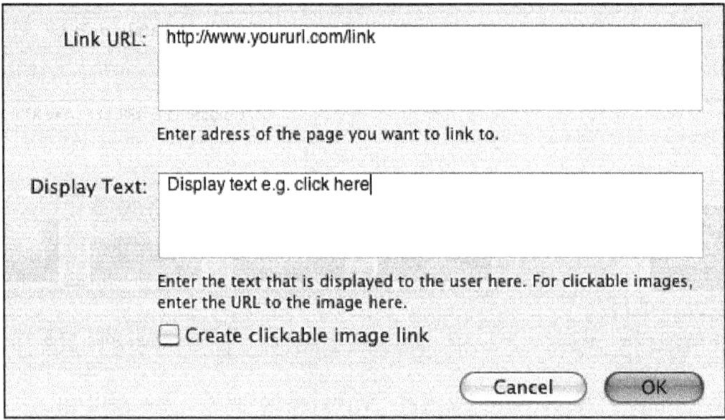

Optionally (instead of the visible link text), you can use a picture for which you'll have to enter the URL as well:

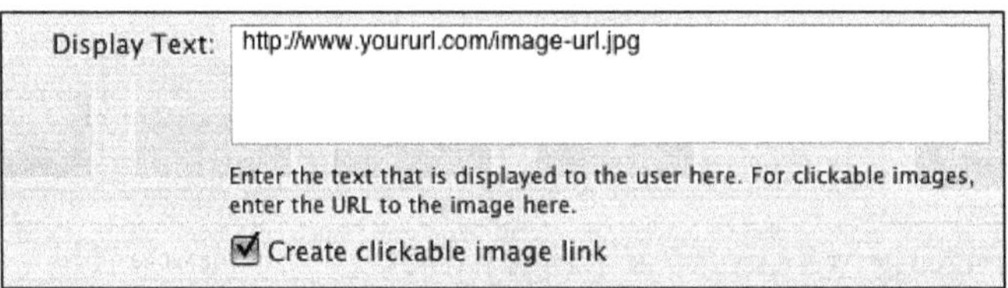

According to your choice a link (text or image) will be added to your auction text:

Convert Description To HTML Now

Only available if the *Convert Description to HTML automatically* checkbox for the selected template is checked. Will convert your text formatting to HTML right away and replace the contents of the description field with the resulting HTML code. Use this menu command to fine tune to generated HTML before it is uploaded to eBay.

When using a version of GarageSale prior to version 2.2, this menu command cannot be undone.

Choose Listing Design

Will present you with a panel showing thumbnails of the available listing designs. Selecting one of those thumbnails will change every selected auction template to use that listing design.

Listing Design

Use the submenu of this menu item to change the design template for all selected templates instantly.

Choose Primary Category

This menu item opens GarageSale category browser and lets you change the primary eBay category for all selected auction templates at once.

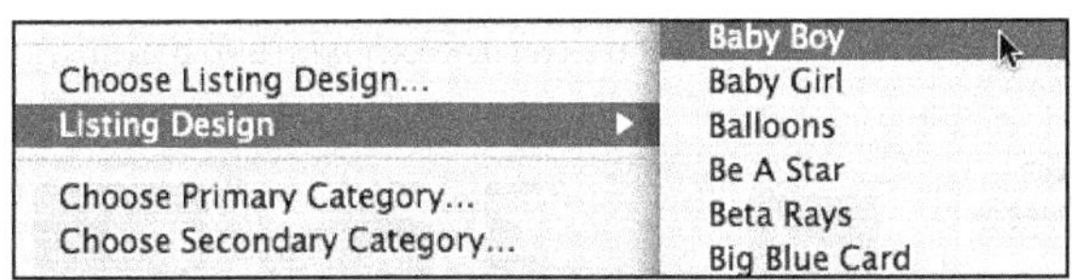

Chose Secondary Category

This menu item opens GarageSale category browser and lets you change the secondary eBay category for all selected auction templates at once.

Edit Payment Options

Invokes the payment options window and lets you change the accepted payment methods for all selected auction templates.

Edit Shipping Options

Brings up the Shipping Options window lets you change the shipping options for all selected auction templates at once. See *Shipping Options* for more information.

Edit Scheduled Time

Brings up a panel that lets you selected the start time for the selected auction templates for use with eBay's scheduler. Unlike GarageSale built-in scheduler eBay's scheduler costs you extra and requires you to start your auctions with GarageSale prior to the auction start time set in this panel. Refer to *Scheduling Auctions* for more information about this topic.

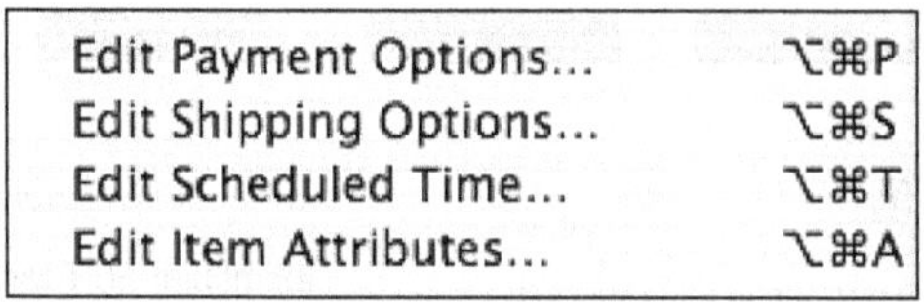

Edit Payment Options...	⌥⌘P
Edit Shipping Options...	⌥⌘S
Edit Scheduled Time...	⌥⌘T
Edit Item Attributes...	⌥⌘A

Edit Item Attributes

Opens a window where you can edit the item attributes (also known as item specifics) for all the selected auction templates, if they are in the same eBay category.

Get Listing Fees from eBay

Retrieves the listing fee for the selected auction templates from eBay if your auctions were to be started right now. Opens a panel displaying a detailed list of how all the auction options add up.

Get Product Information from eBay

Displays a window which can be used to search eBay's product catalog for an item which represents the item your are selling. This menu item is only available if have selected a product enabled eBay category for your item. See Listing with *Pre-filled item information* for more information about this topic.

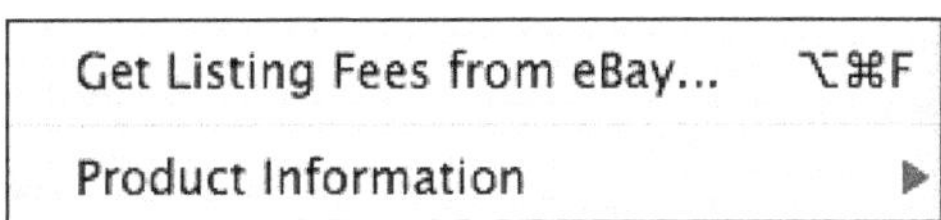

List with eBay Product Information

If a check mark next to the menu item's name, there is an item from eBay's product catalog associated with the selected auction template. Choosing this menu item will turn off the check mark and remove the connection between your auction and eBay's product catalog. See *Listing with Pre-filled item information* for more information about this topic.

CHAPTER 34
IMAGE MENU

The items in this menu will let you work with the auction images of the selected template. Most commands are also available as buttons in *Images* section of the main window.

Add iPhoto Image

Opens a window that displays the contents of your iPhoto Library and lets you add images to be used for the current auction.

This function is also available from the ' ' button at the right of the image list field and can be configured as default action for the *Add Image* button in GarageSale's main toolbar.

Add Camera Image

Use this menu item to import images from your digital camera directly. Just connect your camera to your Mac and select the images you want to add to the current auction template.

This function is also available from the ' ' button at the right of the image list field and can be configured as default action for the *Add Image* button in GarageSale's main toolbar.

You can select the Video Capture Device in *Advanced Preferences*.

Add Image File

Choose this menu item, if you have an existing image file you want to use as an auction image.

This function is also available from the ' ' button at the right of the image list field and can be configured as default action for the *Add Image* button in GarageSale's main toolbar.

Add Image URL

If you already have your auction images uploaded to a web server, invoke this menu item to add the URLs to an existing image to your auction. The URL will be saved with your auction template. When you start your auction, GarageSale will send these URLs to eBay for inclusion in your auction.

This function is also available from the ' ' button at the right of the image list field and can be configured as default action for the *Add Image* button in GarageSale's main toolbar.

Add iSight Image

This menu item lets you take snapshots of your items using your iSight camera (either built-in or connected to your Mac via FireWire).

This function is also available from the ' ' button at the right of the image list field and can be configured as default action for the *Add Image* button in GarageSale's main toolbar.

Mark as Gallery Image

This menu item is only available when an image is selected. It will mark the currently selected image as Gallery Image. This image will appear in the eBay Category listing next to your item when the *All Items including Gallery Preview* tab is chosen by a customer. eBay will charge you extra if you use the Gallery Image option.

Edit

Choosing the *Edit* menu item will bring up GarageSale's *Image Editor*.

This menu item is only available in Mac OS X 10.4 or later.

Rotate Clockwise

Will rotate the selected image 90 degrees in clockwise direction.

Rotate Counter Clockwise

Will rotate the selected image 90 degrees in counter-clockwise direction.

CHAPTER 35
AUCTION MENU

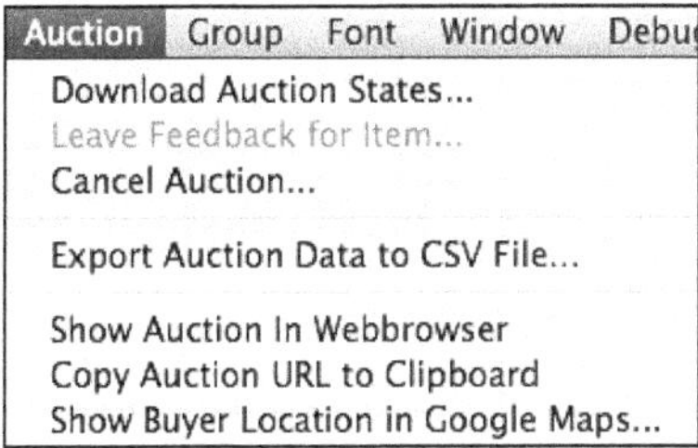

Items from this menu are only available when you switched GarageSale to auction mode.

Download Auction States

This menu item will cause GarageSale to download the most recent state information for your running auctions from eBay. In it's default configuration GarageSale will do this automatically every 60 minutes. You can change the time interval for automatic update in GarageSale's *Tracking Preferences*.

Leave Feedback for Item

Invoking this item will open GarageSale's *Leave Feedback* panel to leave feedback for all the transaction of the selected auctions that you haven't given feedback so far. See *Leaving Feedback* for more information about his.

Cancel Auction

Allows you to cancel/end a running auction.

Export auction data to CSV file

Select this menu item to export the auction data (e.g. buyer address, item number, and listing fee) into a CSV (comma separated value) text file. You can import this file into a database application such as FileMaker Pro or a spreadsheet application like Microsoft Excel.

Show auction in web browser

Will open your Mac's defaults web browser and point it to the eBay item page for the selected auction.

Copy Auction URL to clipboard

Will copy the URL of the selected auction to your clipboard so you can paste into other applications, for instance your e-mail application.

Show Buyer Location in Google Maps

If Tracking is enabled and the buyer address appears in the Inspector > Transactions you can choose this command to see the buyer location in Google Maps.

By default it will be displayed in Firefox (if installed on your system).

Reload Auction (GarageSale 3 only)

This menu item will make GarageSale reload the web page for the selected auction.

CHAPTER 36
GROUP MENU

New Group

Create a new group to better manage your templates.

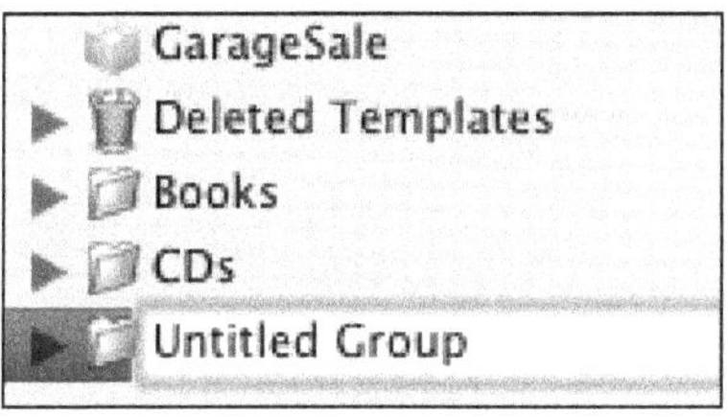

Sort

Your groups will be sorted by name.

CHAPTER 37
Font Menu

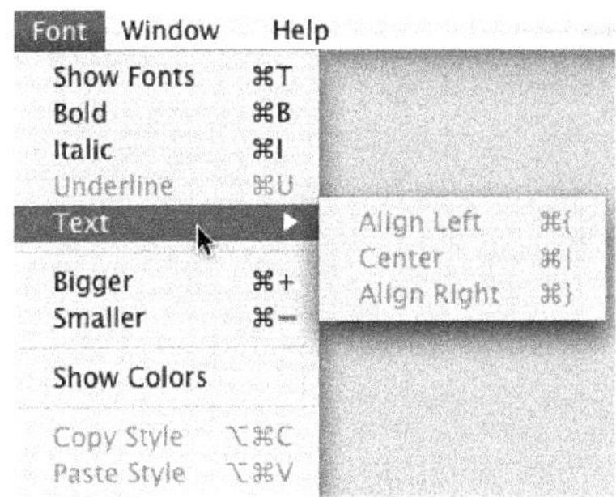

Show Fonts

Will show fonts.

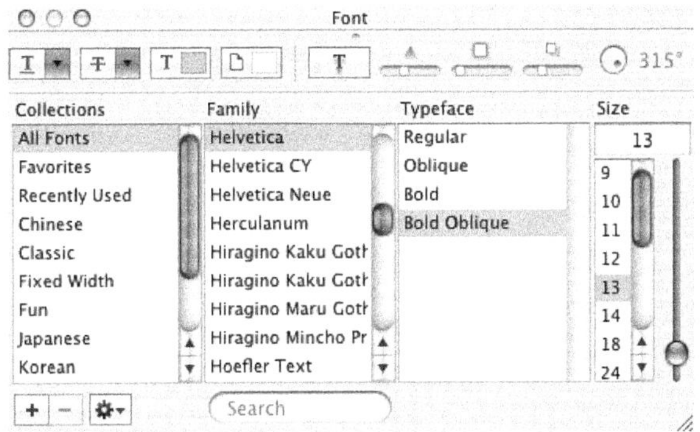

Show Colors

Will show colors.

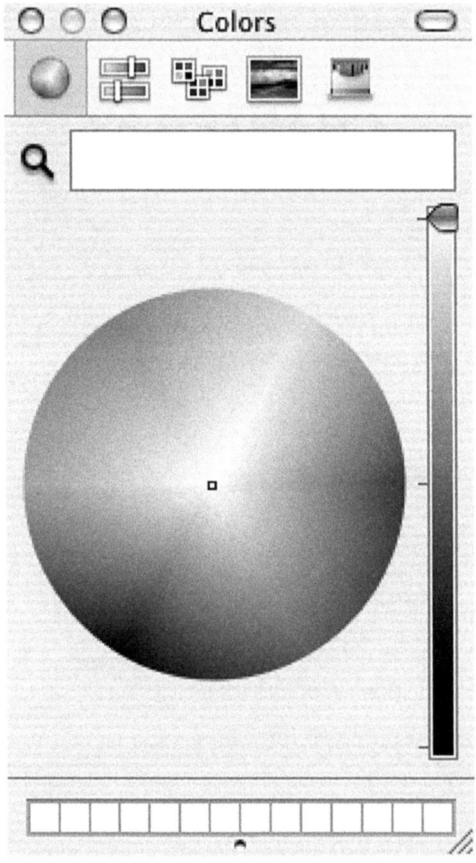

CHAPTER 38
WINDOW MENU

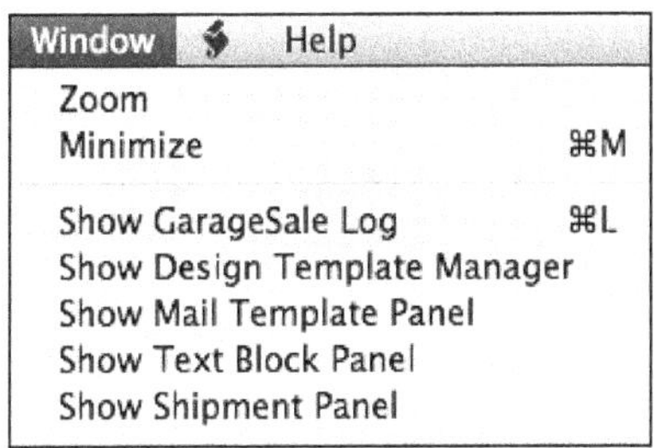

GarageSale Log

In this window you can follow GarageSale's activities, such as starting, stopping, getting transactions, verifying templates, getting updates etc.

Design Template Manager

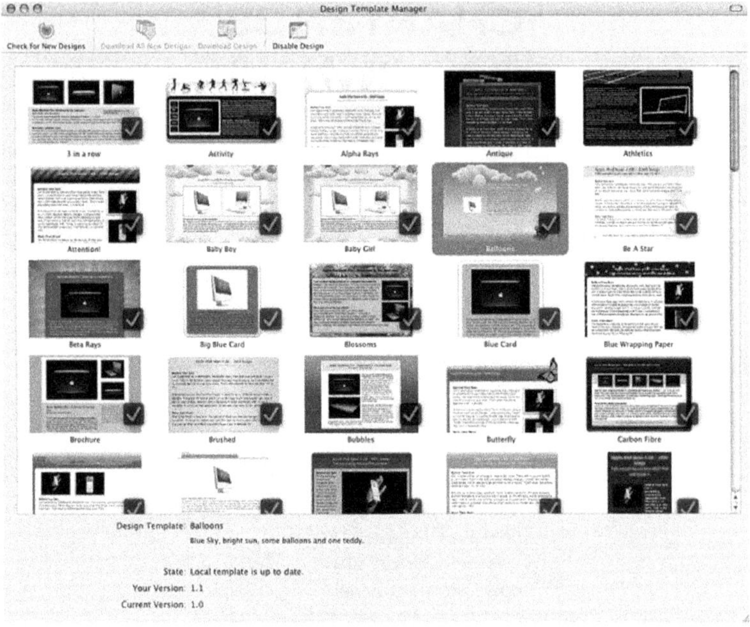

Gives you an overview of available design templates. You can...

- check for new designs
- download new designs
- disable designs you won't use anyway

Mail Template Panel

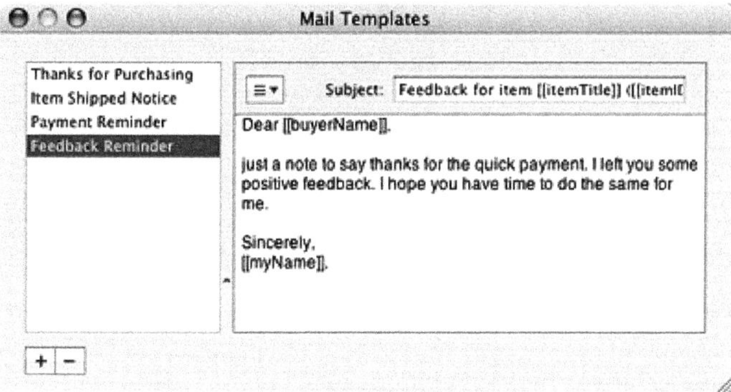

This panel allows you to add, delete and modify mail templates.

Text Block Panel

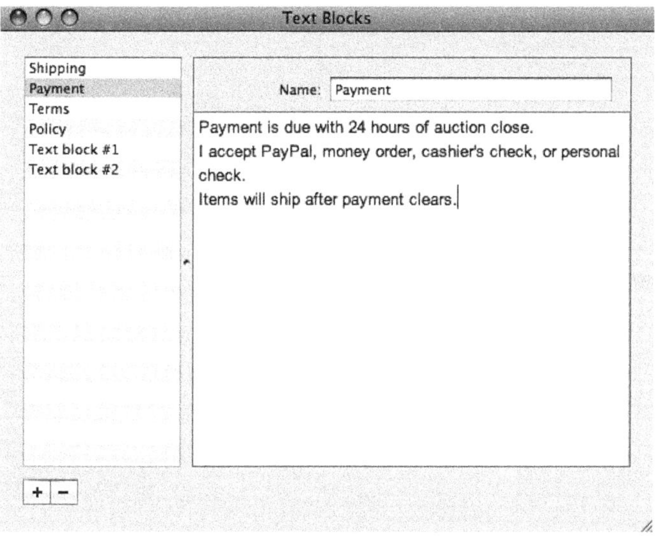

The *Text Block* panel allows you to create re-usable text blocks which you can add to your auction descriptions in *Editor mode* through the "T" drop-down menu. This way you don't have to re-type the same text again and again.

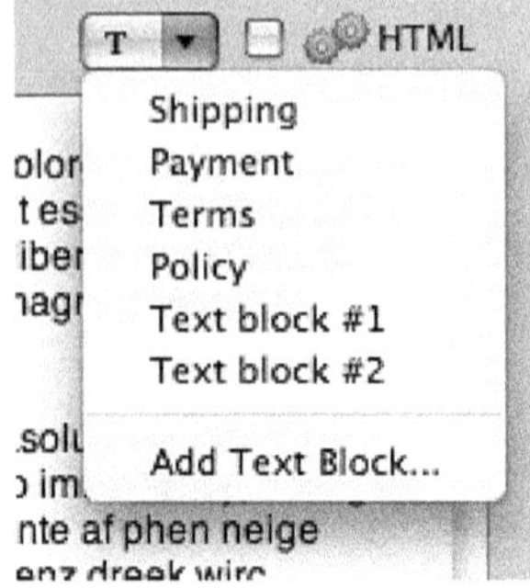

Shipment Panel

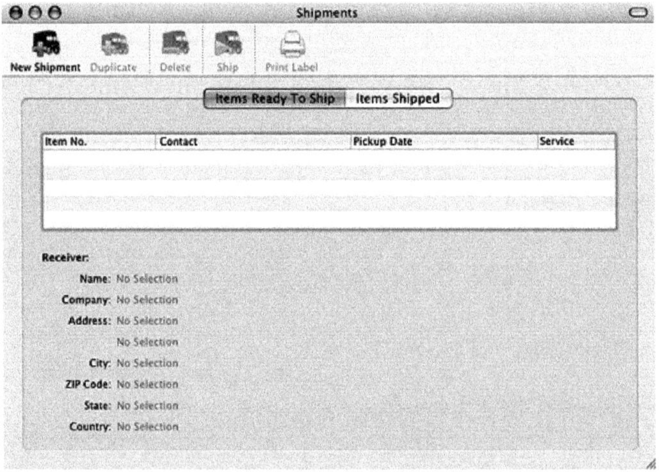

Gives you an overview of shipment status and allows management.

Messages from MyEbay (GarageSale 3 only)

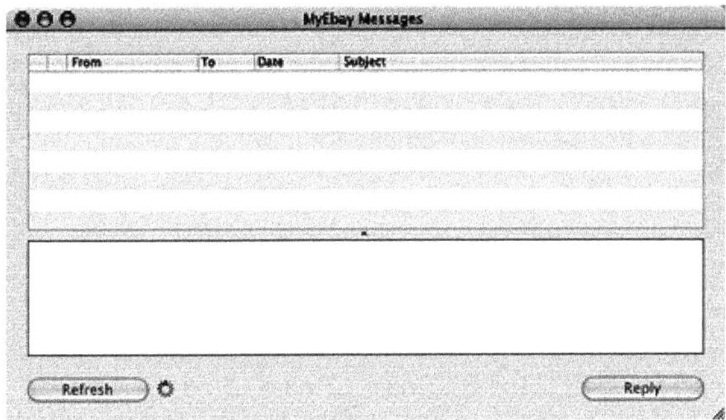

You can access your eBay mail and reply

In *GarageSale 4* and newer you'll find the messages under *Misc* in the main window in the list on the left.

Error Messages

I get an error concerning missing "handling time/ dispatch time."

Due to new eBay policies you have to specify a dispatch time. In GarageSale versions prior to 5.3.2 you can do this in the Inspector>Advanced. To bulk edit multiple auction templates at once, select the templates in the list on the left and choose the *Change dispatch time* script from the *Script* menu.

I get an error my categories or item specifics are wrong.

You've to update the category data. To do so open the GarageSale preferences and update the categories in the Categories tab. (Make sure the correct eBay site is selected in the GarageSale preferences>General.) Back in Template mode check your attribute sets/categories of your template in question.

I get an error concerning my "Authorization Token."

eBay tokens expire automatically after a period of time. To refresh your token, select your account in the GarageSale preferences>Accounts and click on *refresh token.*

When starting an auction I get an error from eBay.

If you don't get a helpful error message from eBay, try to list the exact same auction on the eBay webpage. Sometimes this result in a more informative message than the one eBay provides third party applications like GarageSale with.

I get this error "Cannot open host: user name or password was not accepted for login."

Check your FTP settings in the GarageSale preferences>Image Server and also try it with *use multiple connections* disabled.

I get this error "219—no seller account" when I try to start an auction.

Check your account settings on eBay's website. You need to be registered as a seller. If you're using a recently created ebay account, make sure you list your first item through ebay's website directly. This a restriction by eBay. The following auctions you then can upload through GarageSale.

I get this error "10007 Internal error to the application."

This error is returned by eBay when there is something wrong with their servers. Most likely they are installing a new software version on their machines. Usually this messages goes away after some minutes.

I get this error "240" when I try to start an auction.

This error is returned by eBay when you're using any word or code that eBay does not allow or there's an issue with your seller account.

If a <Message> node is included in the eBay error, you should see a button labeled *More info* at the bottom of the *Error* panel. Clicking on this button should give you an HTML view of the error description. If you don't see the button, there's no <Message> included.

If you're using the terms *money order* or *personal check* in your description or payment instructions, remove it because it is prohibited in most of the categories.

You should also check your seller settings on the "My ebay" site at ebay directly. If this won't help try to list the very same article with the very same description on eBay once. They should give you the exact error message.

Frequently Asked Questions (FAQ)

Installation & Setup

How do I install GarageSale correctly?

Just drag and drop the GarageSale icon to your *applications* folder (or wherever you want) to install the application on your hard drive. Don't start GarageSale directly from the installation disk image!

Why do I have to fetch a token at the eBay site?

GarageSale is a certified eBay client. The only way for certified clients to add listings for your eBay account is via an access token. On the page you are granting GarageSale this eBay token.

Do I have to give you access to my eBay account?

You don't give us access to your account at all! eBays authorization page is a little bit misleading on that. When you agree to the eBay page, you give GarageSale access to your eBay account in form of an access token. This access token is securely stored in your Keychain and not shared with anybody, including us. You control what applications can access your Keychain!

What information will GarageSale share with you?

GarageSale will not share any kind of information about your eBay auctions or eBay activities with us. eBays sign-in page is designed also for web based eBay tools, where your token would be transmitted to the tool provider. Using that token a tool provider could manage your account for you and access your eBay information. GarageSale does not share your token with us, so none of your eBay information is shared.

Usage & Settings

How do I list cars or car parts on eBay Motors?

The eBay Motors site is a different site, like for instance eBay Germany and eBay UK. To list cars or car parts on eBay Motors you have to set the eBay site for your auction template to eBay motors. You can do this in *Advanced settings* of your templates (in versions prior to *GarageSale 2.3* this option was in the Location settings).

If you want to every new template to point to the eBay motors site, you can also set eBay motors as the default site for newly created templates in GarageSale's *Preferences Window*.

Does GarageSale support eBay Stores?

Yes, of course!

How do I add “free shipping”?

Just enter “0.0” into the shipping costs field. eBay converts this to free shipping.

How do I schedule auctions?

To create a new event just select all your templates you want to schedule (or select a folder with templates) and click on *New Event* in the toolbar. You'll then find your new event under *Events* in the list on the left. Open the Inspector window to make your settings and don't forget to activate the event. It's also a good idea to verify the auction template(s).

How do I revise or relist an auction?

Just select the corresponding auction template and click on *Revise* (or *Relist*) in the Inspector window Auctions tab. To bulk revise auctions select *revise running auctions* from the *Template Menu.*

What do all these colors and signs on the template icons stand for?

Different colors and signs symbolize the state of your auctions and auction templates. Have a look at the *GarageSale Legend* for details.

How many eBay accounts can I use with GarageSale?

GarageSale supports multiple accounts. You can add as many accounts as you want!

May I use GarageSale on different eBay sites?

Heck, yeah. In the Inspector window>Advanced, you can use the pulldown menu next to *eBay Site*, in order to select where you would like your listing to run.

Miscellaneous

Is GarageSale's free image service really free?

Absolutely free! You can upload up to 10 images per auction with this service for free. So far only regular auctions are supported (no store items).

Will GarageSale scale down my photos to the right size automatically?

Yes. GarageSale automatically resizes your photos to the maximum size supported by eBay, if you are using eBay's Picture Service for image storage. If you are using GarageSale's free image service, FTP or .Mac you can specify the image size in GarageSale's preferences window.

I bought a boxed version of GarageSale but the key doesn't work?

Don't worry—you have to enter the key from the backside of the manual at http://www.iwascoding.com/Contact/boxed_serial.php to activate the key and to receive a license code for GarageSale.

Why is GarageSale 4 a paid update?

GarageSale 4 is probably the most substantial update in the application's history. For the first time since GarageSale's original release in October of 2004 this update won't be free.

Where can I download older versions?

Older versions of GarageSale can be downloaded from this page: http://www.iwascoding.com/GarageSale/Downloads.html#Older-Versions

The Widget does not work properly?

Please check the following:

- Install the latest widget (Select *Install Widget* from the GarageSale menu)
- Make sure *Tracking* is enabled in the GarageSale preferences
- Allow GarageSaleHelper keychain access when prompted
- Sometimes restarting the Mac does the trick as well.

How do I customize GarageSale's toolbar?

Just right-click (or CTRL-click) on the toolbar and select *Customize Toolbar* to add helpful icons like the Listing Fees icon or the Verify Template icon.

How do I move my GarageSale data to a different Mac?

If you use Apple's Migration Assistant application, which comes with (most/all?) new Macs, it will transfer your GarageSale settings to a new Mac. The first time you use GarageSale on the new machine, you'll be asked if it's OK for your keychain to provide data to GarageSale. That's it!

For other situations, this may help:

GarageSale keeps your data in your home directory under Library/Application Support in a directory called "GarageSale." To make your templates and auctions available on a new Mac, this folder must be copied to the corresponding location on the new Mac. Make sure GarageSale is not running on your old or your new Mac while copying this folder to its new location.

You will also need to enter your license code on your new Mac to unlock the GarageSale demo. To do so, copy your name and your serial number from the original license code e-mail. Depending on the state of the GarageSale installation, you will either need to paste the code into GarageSale's Setup Assistant window or invoke the *Registration* panel from the GarageSale menu manually.

Tutorial Videos

In addition to this manual, iwascoding has a series of very helpful videos that you can doenload or watch online. You can access them at:

http://www.iwascoding.com/GarageSale/Support.html

Video Tutorial: Basics ››› (QuickTime Movie, 4:36 min, 31 MB)

Video Tutorial: Installation ››› (QuickTime Movie, 0:41 min, 3.1 MB)

Video Tutorial: Scheduling Auctions ››› (QuickTime Movie, 0:52 min, 4.1 MB)

Video Tutorial: Revising Auctions ››› (QuickTime Movie, 1:16 min, 7.6 MB)

Video Tutorial: Tips & Tricks ››› (QuickTime Movie, 2:20 min, 16.8 MB)

Other Great Products From iwascoding.com

Free Image Hosting

Store up to ten auction images free of charge on our servers and say Goodbye to eBay's image hosting fees.The quality and number of your auctions pictures is crucial for the success of your auction. With GarageSale Basic you can store up to 10 auction images for regular auctions on our servers without paying image hosting fees to eBay. Of course you can also use eBay's Picture Service (EPS) or your .Mac account for image hosting.

140 Unique Listing Designs

Enhance your listing with one of over 140 listing designs. With each of them you can change how images and description are laid out—giving you more than 1000 unique possibilities. Of course you can also create your own design!

Our free listing designs offer an easy way to make your auction vastly more attractive. GarageSale Basic comes with 140 flexible listing designs for you to choose from. You can pick a listing design by browsing through a CoverFlow-style view.

iPhoto and Aperture integration

The Media Browser lets you import photos from different sources easily. Access all your images from iPhoto and Aperture directly from within GarageSale Basic.—even those used anywhere else on your hard disk! No more copying, pasting or exporting each individual picture from iPhoto. It just works!

.Mac Image Serving

Upload as many images as you like to your .Mac account without paying image hosting fees to eBay.

The quality and number of your auctions pictures is crucial for the success of your auction. While GarageSale Basic allows you to use its Free Image Hosting service or eBay's Picture Service (EPS) for storing your auction images, it can also upload your auction images to your own Mac account. GarageSale Basic will automatically scale your images to the right size before it uploads your images.

Cover Flow

Browse through GarageSale Basic's CoverFlow view and select from 140 free professional listing designs. Each design comes with multiple layout choices!

Full eBay Attribute Support

GarageSale Basic supports eBay's traditional attribute system as well as the new community driven item specifics.

Intuitive Interface

Use GarageSale Basic's mac-like user interface to create auctions conveniently. That means no more waiting on eBay's webserver to guide you trough to several pages step by step. GarageSale Basic is fast, easy to use and comes with everything you need to create and list your auctions.

Spotlight and Quicklook

Search and find your auction templates with Spotlight and preview them quickly with Quicklook (Leopard only).

Give these features a try and test GarageSale Basic for free.

www.iwascoding.com/GarageSaleBasic/index.html

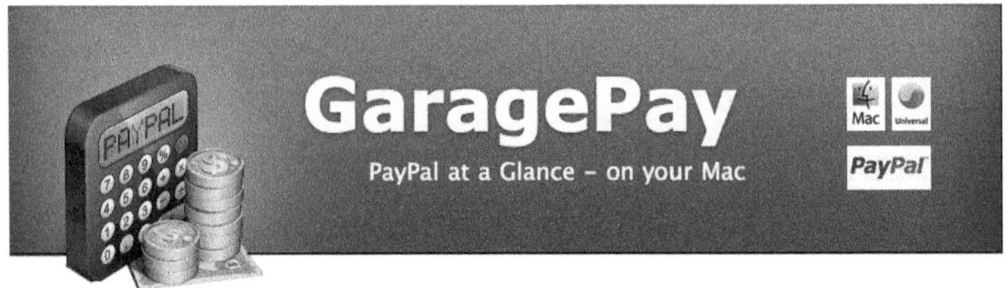

PAYPAL
GaragePay
PayPal at a Glance - on your Mac
Mac
PayPal

Manage Your PayPal Transactions

GaragePay lets you *download, view, search and archive* all your PayPal transactions without having to log into the PayPal website. It handles incoming as well as outgoing money transfers.

Refund Money

One of your customers is not happy? Well it *can* happen. Giving a refund has never been quicker so that you can stop being angry and continue concentrating on your business in no time.

Send Money

With an email like interface GaragePay's way of sending money can be a real time-saver when sending money to a lot of persons.

Powerful CSV Export

Looking for an *easy way* to add PayPal transaction data to your spreadsheet or database? With GaragePay you can *export CSV files* that include all information you need.

Download GaragePay and start with your Paypal account or with a sample database. All that's required is a PayPal account and a Mac running Mac OS X 10.5 Leopard.

Feature Overview

- Download PayPal transactions
- Refund Money
- Send Money
- Smart Folders
- Filter and Find Transactions
- CSV File Export
- Browse and Search Offline
- Multiple Accounts
- Encrypted Database
- Notes
- Address Book Export

Download PayPal transactions

GaragePay downloads all transactions in all your accounts while also updating previously downloaded transactions. Retrieve newly arrived transactions as needed with a simple menu command or keyboard shortcut.

Refund Money

One of your customers is not happy? Well it can happen. Giving a refund has never been quicker so that you can stop being angry and continue concentrating on your business in no time. Partial refunds and adding a message fully supported.

Send Money

With an email like interface GaragePay's way of sending money can be a real time-saver when sending money to a lot of persons. The fees you have to pay are estimated for the most popular currencies.

Smart Folders

Want to keep an eye on payments from the same person? Or transactions in a certain currency? Use *Smart Folder*s to organize your PayPal transactions.

Filter and Find Transactions

Use GaragePay's filter mechanism to find a transaction, a payer's name, his email address, his postal addressor even single words in the transaction message.

CSV File Export

Looking for an easy way to add PayPal transaction data to your spreadsheet or database? Export CSV files that include all information shown in GaragePay's main window. Use *smart folder*s and the filter field to export exactly what you need. Configure the CSV File Export exactly to exactly those fields you need. Use comma, tab or semicolon as separators.

Browse and Search Offline

Since all information resides in GaragePay's own database you can use GaragePay full featured even when don't have an internet connection!

Multiple Accounts

Use as many accounts as you like at the same time.

Encrypted Database

Even if you don't use Apple's File Vault, your financial records are safely locked away in GaragePay's encrypted database.

Notes

Add a note to a transaction to remember what the transaction was about.

Address Book Export

Export the details of a payer to the Address Book.

Give these features a try and test GaragePay for free.

www.iwascoding.com/GaragePay/index.html

SEARCHING EBAY WITH EASE FOR FREE!!

Are you looking for something on eBay but tired of eBay's slow web site? Finally there is a better way! Now you can use a *slick, full-featured client application* for all of your search and purchasing on eBay.

Welcome to **GarageBuy:** An application that looks the way it should (using the Mac's native interface) to help you find and purchase items on eBay.

GarageBuy can *save your eBay searches, tracks your watched auctions and lets you bid on auctions without hassle.*

GarageBuy is Freeware!

GarageBuy can be downloaded and used at no cost. You can download GarageBuy *for free.* All that's required is an eBay account and a Mac running Mac OSX 10.5.

Feature Overview

- Place Bids and Purchase Items directly from within GarageBuy
- First Mac desktop application officially certified by eBay for bidding
- Gallery List View
- Saved Searches
- Visual Tracking of Watched Auctions
- iCal Integration
- Growl Support

Place Bids and Purchase Items directly from within GarageBuy

When you are bidding on an auction that has reached its final phase, GarageBuy will update the current bid, including the highest bidder's name, every few seconds automatically. That means you don't need to hit your browser's reload button until your thumbs bleed.

First Mac desktop application officially certified by eBay for bidding

GarageBuy is the first Mac desktop application officially certified by eBay for bidding and purchasing items on its auctioning platform.

Gallery List View

Are you looking for a special piece of clothing or furniture? With GarageBuy, the days when you needed to open every promising auction to see more than a single picture are over. GarageBuy's Gallery List shows you the most relevant pictures from as many auctions as fit on your screen.

Saved Searches

GarageBuy will save both your searches and found auctions on your Mac's hard drive. For each search, GarageBuy will show the number of the auctions you haven't viewed yet. You can set GarageBuy to hide already viewed items. You can flag items and add them to your watch list, too.

Visual Tracking of Watched Auctions

For every watched auction GarageBuy shows you if you bid on it and whether you are the highest bidder and of course you can see with one glance how much time is left on the auction. The icon of the auction tells you if there's an iCal event for it and if it has already met your threshold.

iCal Integration

GarageBuy integrates perfectly with iCal. For every Watched Auction GarageBuy can automatically create an iCal event with reminder if you choose to do so. Since the iCal calendar database is a fundamental Mac OS feature, events get synched to your mobile devices or other Macs if you have mobileMe. This way you will not miss the end of an auction.

Growl Support

GarageBuy supports the free Growl notification system to display on-screen messages whenever a new item is found or the bid for watched auctions changes.

Search, Track, Bid—Everywhere For FREE!!

GarageBuy for iPhone enables you to *search, track and even bid* on eBay auctions while you are on the road with your iPhone™ or your iPod touch®. Never miss an auction again!

It's built on the experience we gained building our *award-winning* eBay client GarageBuy for Mac OSX®.

International Support:

GarageBuy for iPhone supports *16 different eBay Sites* including eBay US, Canada, Germany and Great Britain. *Happy bidding all around the world!*

Free to use:

GarageBuy touch is freeware!

Download it to your iPhone or iPod touch on Apple's App Store

Feature Overview

- eBay Searching
- Place Bids
- Watch List
- Password Protect your account
- International Support

eBay Searching

Perform eBay searches directly from your iPhone.

Place Bids

Never miss an auction again. Place bids and purchase eBay items from within the GarageBuy for iPhone.

Watch List

See how your watched items are doing. Watched and previously bought items will be imported from My eBay.

Password Protect your account

Optionally protect your eBay account with a password, so nobody can place bids using your iPhone.

International Support

GarageBuy supports 16 different eBay sites. Happy bidding all around the world!

Index

- U -

- V -

- W X Y Z -

For extra help, don't
forget to join the

GarageSale User Group

at Yahoo.com

Browse the messages at the very active GarageSale User Group to see who else uses GarageSale and to meet many helpful GarageSale users there.

http://tech.groups.yahoo.com/group/GarageSale_Users/

CPSIA information can be obtained
at www.ICGtesting.com
Printed in the USA
BVHW01s0821070118
504645BV00023B/737/P

9 781934 757918